Ireland's Independence, 1880–1923

The road to Ireland's independence is one of the most fascinating yet complicated periods in Irish history. This timely introduction presents a clear, balanced account of the momentous events from 1880 leading up to the formation of the Irish Free State in 1922.

Ireland's Independence, 1880–1923 examines the political, social and cultural factors which gave rise to the Free State and the state of Northern Ireland. Beginning with the Gaelic Revival from 1880 to 1910, Walsh guides the reader through the events of the Easter Rising in 1916, the Anglo-Irish War, the Treaty in 1922 and the subsequent Civil War.

Oonagh Walsh is Lecturer in History at the University of Aberdeen.

INTRODUCTIONS TO HISTORY

Edited by David Birmingham

This series of introductions to widely studied and newer areas of the undergraduate history curriculum provides short, clear, self-contained and incisive guides for the student reader.

Introductions to History

Series Editor: David Birmingham
Professor of Modern History, University of Kent at Canterbury

A series initiated by members of the School of History at the University of Kent at Canterbury

Ireland's Independence, 1880–1923

Oonagh Walsh

London and New York

First published 2002
by Routledge
11 New Fetter Lane, London EC4P 4EE

Simultaneously published in the USA and Canada
by Routledge
29 West 35th Street, New York, NY 10001

Routledge is an imprint of the Taylor & Francis Group

Typeset in Sabon and Gill Sans by BC Typesetting, Bristol
Printed and bound in Great Britain by
TJ International, Padstow, Cornwall

British Library Cataloguing in Publication Data
A catalogue record for this book is available from the British Library

Library of Congress Cataloging in Publication Data
Walsh, Oonagh.
    Ireland's independence, 1880–1923/Oonagh Walsh.
    p.   cm. – (Introductions to history)
Includes bibliographical references (p.) and index.
    1. Ireland – History – Autonomy and independence movements.
2. Nationalism – Ireland – History – 20th century. 3. Nationalism –
Ireland – History – 19th century. 4. Ireland – History – Civil War,
1922–1923. 5. Ireland – History – Easter Rising, 1916. 6. Ireland –
History – 1901–1910. 7. Ireland – History – 1910–1921. 8. Ireland –
History – 1837–1901. I. Title. II. Introductions to history
(New York, N.Y.)
DA960.W27 2001
941.508 – dc21   2001041611

ISBN 0–415–23950–8 (hbk)
ISBN 0–415–23951–6 (pbk)

For my daughter, Dearbhla

Contents

Chronology of key events

1880

March–April	General election.
May	Parnell becomes Chairman of the Irish Parliamentary Party.

1881

31 January	Ladies' Land League launched in Ireland.
22 August	Land Law (Ireland) Act.
13 October	Arrest of Parnell.
18 October	'No Rent' Manifesto issued from Kilmainham Gaol.

1882

2 May	Release of Parnell.
6 May	Phoenix Park murders.

1884–1885

Franchise reforms took place which tripled the British electorate.

1885

November–December	General election. The Irish Parliamentary Party won every seat in areas with a Catholic majority, which gave it every seat in the southern provinces bar the two Dublin University seats, and half of those in Ulster.

1886
8 June   Gladstone's Home Rule Bill defeated.
23 October   'Plan of Campaign' announced.

1890
November   O'Shea divorce hearing – Parnell named as co-
                        respondent.
December   Irish Parliamentary Party splits.

1891
6 October   Death of Parnell.

1892
16 August   Foundation of the National Literary Society.

1893
31 July   Gaelic League formed.
2 September   Gladstone attempts to introduce another
                        Home Rule Bill – defeated by House of
                        Lords, 9 September.

1899
Arthur Griffith becomes founder-editor of the *United Irishman*.

1900
30 January   John Redmond becomes leader of the reunited
                        Irish Parliamentary Party.
April   Queen Victoria's visit to Ireland.
30 September   Arthur Griffith founds Cumann na nGaedheal.

1903
July/August   Edward VII makes his coronation visit to
                        Ireland.
14 August   Wyndham Land Act receives third reading,
                        and is passed.

1906
January   Liberals returned to power.

1908

September   Sinn Féin ('Ourselves') formally founded.

29 December   The Irish Transport and General Workers'
                   Union founded by Jim Larkin and James
                   Connolly.

1909

29 April   Lloyd George's 'People's Budget' rejected by
                   House of Lords, 30 November.

1910

21 February   Carson becomes leader of the Irish Unionists.

6 May   Accession of George V. Changes made to the
                   Royal Declaration of Accession which
                   removed attacks on the Mass and on the
                   adoration of the Virgin Mary as 'superstitious
                   and idolatrous'.

1911

18 August   The Parliament Act passed – amended the
                   House of Lords veto to a two-year power of
                   suspension, thereby opening the way to
                   Home Rule.

July   Visit of King George to Dublin.

1912

11 April   Third Home Rule Bill presented to House of
                   Commons.

28 September   Solemn League and Covenant signed by almost
                   220,000 men in Ulster.

1913

30 January and   Home Rule Bill defeated in House of Lords.
15 July

31 January   Ulster Volunteer Force founded.

August   Dublin lock-out.

19 November   James Connolly founds the Irish Citizen Army
                   to protect Dublin workers.

25 November   The Irish Volunteers formed.

4 December   Ban imposed on the import of arms.

1914

20 March	Curragh Mutiny.
24–5 April	Larne gun-running.
26 July	Howth gun-running.
15 September	Home Rule Bill placed on Statute books but suspended for the duration of the war.
20 September	Redmond's Woodenbridge speech.
24 September	Split in Irish Volunteers.

1915

June	Supreme Council of the Irish Republican Brotherhood establishes a Military Committee consisting of Patrick Pearse, Joseph Plunkett and Eamon Ceannt.
29 July	Douglas Hyde resigns as President of the Gaelic League.
1 August	O'Donovan Rossa's funeral, Dublin.

1916

3 April	Pearse orders Irish Volunteers to prepare for manoeuvres on 23 April (Easter Sunday).
20 April	*Aud* arrives at Tralee with arms for Volunteers.
21 April	Roger Casement captured at Banna Strand.
23 April	Eoin MacNeill countermands Pearse's orders.
24 April	Easter Monday – the start of the Easter Rising.
29 April	Surrender of Rebels.
3–12 May	Execution of fifteen rebel leaders.

1917

15 February	Election of Count Plunkett in Roscommon by-election for Sinn Féin.
July–April 1918	Irish Convention meets, without success.
Sinn Féin Ard Fheis	de Valera elected President, and party pledged to Republic.

1918

December	Election brings a massive victory for Sinn Fein. The party captures seventy-three seats to the Irish Parliamentary Party's six, but abstains

from Westminster, establishing Dáil Éireann instead.

1919

21 January	First meeting of Dáil Éireann, and ambush at Soloheadbeg.
1 April	de Valera elected President of Dáil Éireann. Dáil Éireann declared illegal.

1920

January	Recruitment of first Black and Tans.
21 February	Government of Ireland Bill introduced in House of Commons, passed on December 23.
20 March	Murder of Tomas MacCurtain.
July	Recruitment begins for Auxiliary Division.
9 August	Restoration of Order in Ireland Act.
20 September	Sack of Balbriggan.
28 September	Sack of Mallow.
25 October	Death of Terence MacSwiney.
21 November	'Bloody Sunday'. Fourteen suspected British intelligence officers shot in Dublin; Black and Tans fire on crowd at Croke Park; twelve killed.
11–12 December	Sack of Cork.
23 December	Government of Ireland Act.

1921

21 January	Start of government policy of reprisals.
13 May 13	Nominations for parliaments established by Government of Ireland Act – clean sweep by Sinn Féin.
22 June	King George V visits Belfast to open the new Northern Ireland Parliament.
11 July	Truce between British and Irish forces.
16 August	Second Dáil Éireann meets.
11 October	Irish delegation travels to London to discuss terms of agreement for peace.
6 December	Anglo-Irish Treaty signed in London.
14 December	Dáil Éireann begins debates on the Treaty.

1922

7 January	Dáil Éireann approves Treaty by sixty-four votes to fifty-seven.
9 January	de Valera resigns as President of Dáil Éireann; Arthur Griffith elected in his place.
7 April	Special Powers Act passed by Northern Ireland Parliament.
14 April	Anti-Treaty forces under Rory O'Connor seize the Four Courts.
20 May	Pre-election pact between Michael Collins and de Valera.
31 May	Royal Ulster Constabulary established.
16 June	General election – pro-Treaty candidates secure majority of seats.
28 June	Provisional government attacks Four Courts.
12 August	Death of Arthur Griffith.
22 August	Death of Michael Collins.
September	Third Dáil meets.
25 October	Constitution of the Free State approved.
15 November 1922 –2 May 1923	Execution of seventy-seven irregulars.

1923

10 April	Death of Liam Lynch.
24 May	Civil war ends.

The nineteenth-century context, 1800–1880

The year 1800 marked not just the start of a new century, but the start of a new relationship between Britain and Ireland. The end of the eighteenth century had seen a relatively brief but very bloody rebellion in 1798, and the presence of French troops in Ireland, drawn to the assistance of the rebels, posed an obvious threat to British security. In addition to other political and economic factors, the uprising helped to persuade many British, and indeed Irish, politicians that Ireland should be drawn more closely into the heart of British government. The century therefore opened with a dramatic adjustment in Anglo-Irish relations through the Act of Union of 1800, which took effect on 1 January 1801. Under this legislation, Ireland lost her Dublin Parliament, and Irish members instead took their seats at the Westminster body. The passage of the Act of Union had not been smooth, and was regarded by few as an ideal solution to recent turbulent events such as the 1798 rebellion. Indeed, its lack of impact, so far as containing dissent is concerned, may be seen by the fact that in 1803 another rebellion took place. Although small scale and easily suppressed, it was an indication that militantism had not been eliminated by union. It did nevertheless have a significant impact upon how the country was governed. Far from increasing democratic rule, the Act of Union, and the unambiguous siting of political power at Westminster instead of Dublin, further distanced the majority of Irish people from the process of government.

In theory, the Act of Union should have given the majority of Irish citizens a fairer share in government – the eighteenth-century Irish House of Commons represented for practical purposes only the land-owning members of the Church of Ireland (Anglicans).

Roman Catholics did not have the vote, and Protestant groups other than Anglicans (in particular Presbyterians) also had limitations placed upon their political participation. However, the shift to Westminster did not appreciably improve their participation in democratic politics, or further their religious or economic interests. The major part of Irish property was held by a small number of landed families. In the majority of cases these people were Protestant, and for the most part unionist in their politics. They had little in common with the mass of their tenants and employees, and indeed there existed in many cases a deep enmity between the two groups. Moreover, there was legislative discrimination which further deepened the divide. The established church in Ireland was the Church of Ireland, to which all citizens paid dues in the form of tithes, yet it was the religion of the minority. The single largest religious group in Ireland were Roman Catholics, who also made up the majority of landless labourers and tenant farmers, and comprised approximately three-quarters of the population throughout the century. In Ireland, where little large-scale industrialisation had taken place, land was the principal measure of wealth. From the sixteenth century, a series of laws had been enacted, known as the Penal Laws. These created a draconian system whereby non-Anglicans were prohibited from owning more than a strictly limited amount of land, were barred from certain professions, excluded from higher education, and had severely restricted inheritance rights. Although the implementation of the laws had eased over the years, and especially by the late eighteenth century, they remained as a major grievance. Some of the Penal Laws affected Presbyterians as well as Catholics, but Catholics were further discriminated against through the requirement that Members of Parliament take an oath denouncing Catholicism before entering Parliament. This meant that Catholics – the majority of the population – could only be represented by Protestants, and had the practical effect of ensuring that the redress of Catholic grievances was a relatively low priority for Irish parliamentarians. Thus after the Act of Union, when potential for change seemed great, a vigorous campaign to repeal the Penal Laws, and confer basic rights upon the non-Anglican population, took place.

The most important figure in this campaign was Daniel O'Connell, a lawyer from an affluent Catholic family in Kerry. His commitment to Catholic rights, and his detestation of violence, made him a formidable leader of the largest popular movement ever seen in Ireland. He encouraged the peasantry to become actively involved in politics through his Catholic Association, founded in 1823. Although full membership cost a guinea a year, O'Connell launched an Associate membership scheme, costing one penny per month, and such was the popular support that he was able to fund his nationwide political campaign from the proceeds. He pioneered the mass meeting, and is estimated to have addressed a crowd of between 500,000 and 750,000 on one occasion. His activities were closely monitored both by the government and by aspirant nationalist politicians, who, if they did not sympathise with what they regarded as his pacific attitude towards reform, learned valuable lessons in the art of mass mobilisation. O'Connell's campaign came to a successful conclusion in 1829, with the granting of Catholic Emancipation in the Roman Catholic Relief Act, which removed legal prohibitions upon Catholics, but, more importantly, eliminated the required oath for parliamentary participation. This cleared the way for the election of Catholic members, and although change was not as dramatic as followers had hoped – few ordinary Irishmen could realistically afford to stand for high office – it opened the possibility of full political participation.

The transfer of Irish representation to London had other important consequences. With the movement of many Irish landowners to England, where they now perceived both government and society to reside, many Irish estates began to deteriorate. Land agents were appointed, whose principal concern lay in the collection of rents for their employers, and not in the maintenance or improvement of property. In order to ensure a constant stream of funds, agents allowed the steady subdivision of land among tenant farmers, so that much of the Irish economy was precariously dependent upon a base of barely subsistence-level cottiers. These factors would have been dangerous enough in any country, but there were other elements specific to Ireland which made the situation even more alarming.

The stereotype of the Irishman and the potato is long-standing, yet the Irish dependence on this crop came about comparatively recently. It was only in the later eighteenth century that the potato became a central part of the Irish peasant's diet, but once this had been established it drastically altered certain demographic and social trends which were to have serious consequences. The potato was a remarkable crop – capable of producing a high yield on poor soil, and extremely nutritious, even without supplements of other foods. Thus the potato became the favoured food among the poorest of the Irish, those usually described as the cottiers, and also an important animal feed. Once assured of this cheap, easily grown staple, Irish marriage patterns changed. Instead of having to wait a considerable time until land, or a lease of land, became available, young men and women could marry earlier if they could secure even the smallest patch of ground on which to cultivate potatoes. Tenants with large lands subdivided their holdings among poorer individuals, thereby increasing their own incomes as well as those of their landlords, and parents in turn allowed their already inadequate holdings to be divided among their children in order to allow them to marry. Under normal circumstances, when a landlord resided on his estate and maintained a tight hold upon his tenantry, such an unstable situation would not have been allowed to develop. However, with large numbers of landlords based permanently in London (the so-called absentee landlords), and their agents in Ireland concerned only with the payment of rents, the division and subdivision of land was allowed to spread largely unchecked.

The dependence of the Irish upon the potato was clearly a dangerous trend. Just how dangerous was to be proven in the years 1845–1850, when intermittent blight struck the country and destroyed what was for many their sole food supply. The ensuing famine and misery is beyond description. By 1855 the population had dropped by two million, lost to starvation, disease and emigration. Between 1850 and 1900 a further two million individuals emigrated to North America, Australia and Britain, and few of them returned. When famine first struck in Ireland, the British government had made efforts, particularly under Sir Robert Peel, to initiate relief measures for the starving, but when Lord John Russell became Prime Minister in June 1846, governmental attitudes towards Ireland underwent a drastic change. Faithful to the economic philosophy of *laissez-faire*, whereby no government interference in economic matters should take place, Russell's cabinet was seen to preside over the decimation of the Irish population in an especially heartless and brutal manner. Such relief as was available required either the complete abandonment of property and goods, and entry to the workhouse, or else scanty employment on largely pointless work schemes, building what became known as the 'Famine

Roads' which notoriously led nowhere – a perhaps appropriate image for the period. The powerlessness of the people, and the apparent indifference of the government to their sufferings, left a dangerous legacy of anger and resentment that was to shape political developments in the second half of the nineteenth century.

Although the Famine had exposed the serious shortcomings of the Irish agricultural system, harsh lessons did not appear to have been learned. Although some landowners made efforts to modernise – a strategy which in some cases involved removing tenants from land and using it for the more profitable business of cattle rearing – many lapsed into the old system of leasing undeveloped land, and allowing their tenants to continue with outmoded and inefficient farming methods. There had however been considerable shifts in land-ownership, with a growing class of Catholic farmers and an almost total elimination of cottiers. Several major landlords had disappeared entirely, either bankrupt as a result of their efforts to provide Famine relief for their tenants, or having taken advantage of new legislation which allowed them to sell their lands, despite the often large debts entailed upon them. Marriage patterns also changed dramatically, with men in particular marrying much later in life, and a considerable proportion of the population remaining unmarried. Far from the pre-Famine practice of subdivision of land among several offspring, Irish farmers now favoured leaving all land and property to one child, and sought as far as possible to use marriage as a means of consolidating and enlarging holdings. This left considerable numbers of young men and women with the unattractive options of either remaining on the family farm as unpaid and unmarried labourers, or emigrating in the hope of brighter prospects abroad.

It has been said that the most enduring legacy of the Great Famine was psychological rather than physical, and this is probably true. There are certainly echoes in Ireland of the sorts of responses exhibited by survivors of the Holocaust, as direct survivors of the Famine, and their descendants, appeared to react against the types of behaviour common to the pre-Famine period. Irish society became more conservative with, for example, rates of illegitimacy dropping sharply. Attendance at church rose dramatically, and support for church teaching became stronger. Indeed, one of the most remarkable features after 1850 was the sharp increase in the professed religious in Ireland. Although many religious orders had previously established houses in the country, their ranks swelled in the second half of the nineteenth century, and entry to a convent or to the priesthood became a source of pride for Irish families and reinforced religious conformity.

If the moral life of the Irish became more conformist in the post-Famine years, the same could not be said for politics. A radicalism, which would eventually find full expression in the Land War of the late nineteenth century, had begun to take shape in the 1840s. At the start of the decade, O'Connell had launched the National Repeal Association, an organisation dedicated to the repeal of the Act of Union. By this time, O'Connell's hold on the Irish people was less strong than it had been in the heady days of Catholic Emancipation, but he remained capable of persuading many of the benefits of breaking with Britain. Most importantly, he attracted the support of a dynamic group of radicals led by Thomas Davis, John Blake Dillon and Charles Gavan Duffy, who called themselves 'Young Ireland', and joined the Repeal Association in 1841. Their organisation was non-sectarian; indeed, it actively advocated the participation of Catholics and Protestants in the movement, an ambition reflected in the mixed religions of its leadership. The Young Irelanders sought not just the Union's repeal, but a drastic shake-up of Irish society, including land-ownership, education and politics, ideas they expounded in their newspaper the *Nation*, which gained an influential and articulate readership throughout the country. Within just two years, however, the Young Irelanders were clashing regularly with O'Connell, believing that his strategies were outmoded and ineffectual, and his policy too bound to a rigid Catholicism ever to achieve success. More important however were their differing attitudes towards the use of violence. Although the Young Irelanders did not necessarily advocate militantism as a policy, they refused to reject it as a possible strategy, which clashed directly with O'Connell's dearest principles of pacifism, and was entirely unacceptable to his vision of the Repeal Association. It did however provide a convenient means through which he could shed the Young Irelanders, whom he increasingly regarded as a threat to his authority. In July 1846 he proposed a resolution to the Repeal Association which excluded the use of violence. The Young Irelanders resigned, and the schism appeared total.

These changes took place against the terrible backdrop of the Famine. As it progressed, and O'Connell's Association appeared unable to provide either clear leadership or to extract any concessions from government, the Young Irelanders determined upon drastic action. To this end they launched an unsuccessful rebellion in July 1848, which failed through a combination of poor planning, lack of support from the enfeebled peasantry, and their own general reluctance, despite their rhetoric, to encourage widespread violence. However, the 1848 rebellion had several important consequences. It popularised the notion of complete independence from Britain, it provided an example of militant nationalism, and it showed how religion, usually so divisive in Irish politics, could in fact be a source of strength, allowing the whole nation to claim, in the words of Wolfe Tone, 'the common name of Irishman'.

Some of these effects were visible sooner than others. Two contrary movements developed out of the events of 1848. One was the emergence of a distinct Irish Party at Westminster, and the other was 'the Fenians' (a catch-all phrase for nationalists and republicans in the mid-nineteenth century, especially those of a militant persuasion). The first of these took shape under the guidance of Charles Gavan Duffy, who after 1848 became increasingly convinced that a united front of Irish members at Westminster was the best way of ensuring political advance. Gavan Duffy also encouraged the formation of the Tenant League (1850) which was intended to unite tenants with grievances against unfair rents and other issues into a body that would be capable of forcing landlords to negotiate. Although neither of Gavan Duffy's initiatives met with immediate success, the model he outlined was to be utilised, with considerable impact, in the 1880s. The Fenians followed a somewhat different route. After 1848, those not immediately imprisoned fled the country, some to America, where they found a ready audience for revolutionary rhetoric among Famine emigrants, and some to France, including James Stephens, who was to return to Ireland in 1856 and coordinate the new revolutionary movement – the Irish Republican Brotherhood (IRB). A secret society, the IRB had strong support from America, and although the organisation proved surprisingly vulnerable to infiltration by government spies, it endured. Fenian activity varied over the century, but was to come into its own in the independence movement of the 1910s and 1920s.

The Famine had left another legacy, and it was one which was to overshadow Irish politics into the twentieth century. There was a commonly held belief that the British government had made little effort to alleviate the disaster, and that they had even connived in ensuring mass starvation and migration. Embedded deep in folk memory was the sight of ships loaded with grain leaving Irish ports for English markets. The fact that many Irish landlords saw the Famine as a means of turning their land over to the more profitable business of grazing cattle, rather than raising crops, seemed further proof that English and Anglo-Irish interests would always be contrary to Irish. The large-scale migration to North America in particular created a ready-made political constituency for Irish radicalism. Generations of Irish-Americans were raised in the certainty that the British government had enacted a genocidal system during the Famine years, and they were therefore more than willing to fund militant Irish organisations which sought to secure Irish independence. The Great Famine of 1845–1850 had been the ultimate test of the Union, and it was a test which Britain was seen to fail. Contemporary commentators noted that, had a similar disaster struck England, people would not have been allowed to suffer and die in such numbers. Thus many Irish felt that despite the rhetoric of equality implied by the union, Ireland remained very much the poor relation. This was an attitude which was to encourage efforts towards breaking that relationship over the next seventy years.

CHAPTER ONE

Culture, land and politics, 1880–1900

It has been said that whenever the English came close to solving the so-called Irish question, the Irish changed the question. This is not quite true, but what is clear throughout the 1880s is that each element in the Anglo-Irish relationship sought a different objective, and interpreted political change in very different ways. The late nineteenth century saw the emergence of clear, and often antagonistic, political groups in Ireland which enjoyed varying levels of support within Westminster. In addition, there were many other organisations whose brief was to encourage a sense of Irish pride through a revival of language, culture and sport, but which shaded into more explicitly political movements, often against their will. The determining element in this period was Home Rule and the varied reactions to it, but the most dramatic development of the period was the rise of the Irish Parliamentary Party, and the emergence of Charles Stewart Parnell as its leader.

Home Rule – a measure of independent government for Ireland – suggested very different possibilities to different groups. Although it had been part of Anglo-Irish debates for many years, it did not take concrete form until the late 1860s and early 1870s. In 1870 the Home Government Association was founded, and in 1873 the Home Rule League was created, largely taking over from the earlier organisation. Although committed to reform within Westminster, the Home Rule Party, as the parliamentary representatives were known, displayed an increasing willingness to use tactics of obstruction in order to force consideration of the Irish cause. Central to this strategy was Charles Stewart Parnell, a Protestant landowner from Wicklow, elected for County Meath in 1875. Parnell was an ambitious and intelligent leader, one of the first to attempt to unite the two strands of constitutionalism and militantism in Irish politics in order to secure reform. He clashed with the party leader Isaac Butt, who disapproved of what he saw as Parnell's dangerous irreverence towards parliamentary procedure, but Parnell secured increasing support among the more aggressive party members, as well as radical elements among the Fenian movement throughout Britain and the United States. In May 1880 Parnell was elected Chairman of the Irish Parliamentary Party, as the Irish Home Rule members at Westminster were now known, and immediately began to forge the party into a cohesive body focused specifically upon the goal of Home Rule. An accomplished parliamentarian, Parnell swiftly realised that success would depend upon association with the other key reform movement in Ireland – the Land League.

The National Land League had been established in 1879 by Michael Davitt in Co. Mayo as a radical response to the deepening crisis in land issues in Ireland. The position of the Irish peasant, especially in the west, was as bad as it had been since the Great Famine, and for largely the same reason. Between 1877 and 1879 the potato crop failed, and this, allied to an economic slump, resulted in failure of rental payments and large-scale evictions. Davitt's personal circumstances had inclined him towards radicalism in any case, but in the autumn of 1879 he managed to persuade Parnell to become President of the Irish National Land League, the organisation formed as a response to the support among tenants to the Mayo initiative. This was a hugely significant moment. Although Parnell was deeply interested in land reform, and in improving the lot of the Irish tenant, he was not, at this stage, a believer in the sort of radical peasant proprietorship which Davitt favoured. Parnell also had ambitions which went beyond mere transfers of land, namely Home Rule. His assumption of the presidency therefore placed him at the head of the two most powerful mass movements in Ireland – the Land League and the Irish Parliamentary Party – which sought to transform land occupancy and national government forever.

Although this strategy might appear logical enough from our distant perspective, it was a risky one for Parnell. The slogan of the Land League was 'the land of Ireland for the people of Ireland' – a direct threat to the position of Irish landlords, and an implied threat to national security. Although the Land League did not officially espouse violence as a means of securing tenant rights, it was an ever-present element among the ordinary members. The League's most useful weapon, and one which it encouraged followers to use, was boycott. (The word boycott derives from the case of Captain Charles Boycott, a land agent and farmer from Co. Mayo, whose tenants refused to gather his harvest in September 1880. Unionist labourers were brought in, at great expense, from Counties Monaghan and Cavan, but the effectiveness of the strategy had been proven to the League's satisfaction: thereafter, the policy, and the name, became common.) Tenants were advised to refuse their labour to landlords who demanded excessive rents, and to boycott anyone who took land from which another had been evicted. However, within a short period of time more violent methods of indicating disapproval emerged, and attacks upon persons and property, especially livestock, increased. Parnell was a constitutional nationalist, and any taint of illegal militant activity would damage his parliamentary career. Moreover, Parnell was himself a landowner, and wished as far as possible to protect the interests of that class, while ameliorating tenant grievances. Yet to allow anyone else to assume the Presidency of the League was to run the risk of eroding his popular power base, and alienate support from the Irish Parliamentary Party. Ironically, although he did not advocate the agrarian violence which frequently accompanied Land League activity, it became a useful element in his negotiations with the British government, and made government officials less critical of his leadership. His British parliamentary colleagues may have had reservations regarding his ultimate intentions for Ireland, but he provided the only acceptable point of contact between Westminster and the mass of the Irish people. It was believed, not entirely correctly, that Parnell could control the agrarian movement, and this was to prove extremely valuable when the campaign moved into a more violent phase.

One major grievance, as far as land reformers were concerned, was the regulation of rents, and another was land-ownership. Tenants could be subject to the whims of landlords, and depended upon custom rather than law for their rights. There was therefore a good deal of support for widespread land purchase, although there was much argument over whether this should be compulsory, or voluntary and gradual. Tenants throughout the country, but particularly in the west, increasingly adopted boycott and intimidation against landlords to secure an improvement in their economic position. The government responded on two fronts: in 1881 the Land Law (Ireland) Act was passed, which allowed for the adjudication of rent levels, limited the landlord's right to evict, and gave tenants the right of Free Sale. The second initiative was an attempt to crush the Land League by the suppression of the organisation and the large-scale arrest and imprisonment of activists, including, in October 1881, Parnell himself. He predicted that his imprisonment would remove any restraint as far as land agitation was concerned, and this belief did appear to be borne out. From Kilmainham Gaol, Parnell issued a call for a rent strike, a strategy which suggested that large-scale violence and disruption must inevitably follow. In fact, it would appear that Parnell was more concerned with maintaining the threat of violence rather than actually provoking it, for the actions of the body which assumed responsibility for coordinating land protest were met with alarm by both the Land League and the government.

It was to be women who took the land agitation movement into a new and radical phase. The male leadership of the Land League decided that in their enforced absence, Land League activities would be dealt with by what was literally its sister organisation, the Ladies' Land League. This organisation had been established by Fanny Parnell, sister of Charles Stewart, while in America in the autumn of 1880. Despite Fanny's wish to see an Irish branch established under the leadership of her sister Anna, this move was resisted until Michael Davitt took the simple, if rather arrogant, step of announcing the organisation of a Ladies' Land League in Ireland, headed by Anna. This rather inauspicious beginning was an unfortunate indication of things to come, as the women played 'catch-up' with male policy, and were excluded from the process of decision making. Anna, somewhat reluctantly, came to Dublin in December 1880, and the women's organisation was set up in the same premises as that of the Land League. The purpose of the Ladies' Land League was to support evicted tenants, and to work to prevent land-grabbing. To this end they were to finance the construction of wooden shelters for evicted families, and disburse funds to the dependants of those imprisoned for withholding rent. As far as the Ladies' Land League was concerned, this policy was a mandate for radical action. Within a relatively short time, however, it became clear that the Land League had intended them to be a symbol of resistance rather than a practical body, a misconception which was to prove fatal to relations between the two organisations.

When Anna Parnell began the task of organising the Ladies' Land League, she turned first to the existing Land League structures. To her alarm, she found an almost total shambles. Instead of the nation-wide network of branches which she had been led to believe existed, there was instead an extremely uneven patchwork of associations with wildly differing degrees of efficiency. It soon became clear that in many places the Land League had done no more than make rhetorical speeches about resistance and solidarity, while offering little practical support. There was no consistency with regard to the non-payment of rent, with the result that a coherent strategy to implement rent strikes had never been devised. Thus where the men had been content with the appearance of resistance, the women actively supported a strategy of militant action, one which involved at least verbal, if not physical, encouragement towards agrarian violence. Anna and the other female activists implemented Land League policy in full. The 'No Rent' Manifesto issued by Parnell and his colleagues from Kilmainham Gaol on 18 October 1881 was brought to its logical conclusion, leading to the eviction of tenants and their families. The Ladies' Land League refused to allow grants for the payment of rent, and although they assisted evicted families, they did so where possible in kind rather than in cash, which they feared would simply be used to pay rent. They held demonstrations, observed elections, obstructed rent collectors, and encouraged the boycotting of members of the Royal Irish Con-stabulary, and land agents. It proved to be an expensive policy – the organisation spent £70,000 between October 1881 and May 1882 in relief to evicted families. The women sought to professionalise the land war, and compiled an impressive rent book, detailing estate information from all over the country, which became known as the 'Book of Kells'. Not surprisingly, the Ladies' Land League appeared to violate prevalent Victorian notions regarding appropriate spheres of action for men and women, although in fact what the women had done was simply translate the political rhetoric of the Land League into practical political action, and as a result attracted a good deal of criticism. They were denounced by the main churches for their unfeminine behaviour, and criticised by Land League members for militancy and supposed extravagance. The government, alarmed at the deteriorating situation in Ireland, approached C.S. Parnell in prison. A deal, known as the Kilmainham Treaty, was agreed, whereby the government pledged to address land grievances, including the rent arrears which had grown as a result of recent agitation, and Parnell pledged to accept the 1881 Act as a basis for land reform in Ireland. The treaty was agreed without the knowledge of the Ladies' Land League, and on Parnell's release relations between the two organisations deteriorated badly. Without explanation, the Land League starved the women's organisation of funds, but did not immediately ask it to disband. The reason for this peculiar policy appears to have been a reluctance to be seen to immediately destroy an organisation which had attracted a great deal of attention and support from Irish tenants, but it left the Ladies' Land League in the unenviable position of continuing a policy which they themselves had not devised, but in the face of tacit disapproval from the male leadership. There were personal as well as political consequences from this policy: Anna and Charles quarrelled badly, and did not speak to each other again.

Other events swiftly overtook personal and national difficulties. In May 1882, just four days after Parnell's release from prison, the new Chief Secretary (Lord Frederick Cavendish) and new Under-Secretary for Ireland (Thomas Henry Burke) were murdered in Phoenix Park. There were rumours which attempted to link Parnell with the murders, attempts which were to be publicly rebutted in the Special Commission set up in 1888 to investigate allegations made in *The Times* newspaper about Parnell and other Irish nationalists. Parnell denounced the murders and settled himself to the task of forging the Irish Parliamentary Party into a key political body. He did so by increasingly, though subtly, distancing himself from militant nationalism, although so reserved was he in this regard that his change in strategy went unnoticed by many. Nationally popular, regarded with respect, if not affection, by fellow-Parliamentarians, Parnell emerged as the single most important political figure in the country. In 1886, Gladstone underwent his rather unexpected 'conversion' to Home Rule, a development which appeared to pay tribute to Parnell's political strategies. But looked at from Westminster, events in Ireland formed only a part of a complex series of legal, constitutional and ideological changes which took place during that decade, and indeed before it. For example, the disestablishment of the Church of Ireland, overseen by Gladstone in 1869, was the single most important event for the church in the nineteenth century. However, from Gladstone's perspective, although he had been committed to reform since the 1850s, its real importance lay in providing an experimental model for the disestablishment of the Church of Wales, and even, possibly, that of England. Gladstone's commitment to Home Rule, explicitly expressed from 1886, was similarly part of his drive towards a greater democracy in British politics. In 1884–1885 reforms of the British franchise took place which tripled the electorate, and this consideration of the rights of the broader population partly explains Gladstone's willingness to consider Home Rule for Ireland. However, the Tory Party, led by Lord Salisbury, strenuously opposed even the most moderate concessions for Ireland, believing it would signal the disintegration of British Imperial power. Salisbury feared that Gladstone's plan to grant a limited measure of power to Irish constitutional nationalists would provide an undesirable example to important possessions such as India, in a period in which the major European powers were actually expanding their empires. The general atmosphere in Britain was therefore not conducive to sympathy for Irish nationalism. Furthermore, the Tory philosophy of elite rule, centralised control and unswerving patriotism had a far more popular appeal to the majority of the population than the democratic, conciliatory approach of the Liberals. Allied to an entrenched anti-Catholicism in British society, which was strengthened by what many regarded as the alarming increase of Catholics in the country (the Catholic population in Britain more than doubled to 1,500,000 between 1840 and 1900) the prevailing view was that Home Rule ambitions should be actively discouraged.

If Gladstone was relatively well disposed to moderate nationalism, Salisbury and his Tories were whole-heartedly behind Irish unionists. This latter group emerged as a significant political entity from the late nineteenth century, defined largely by opposition to Home Rule, and a determination to maintain the union between Britain and Ireland intact. Although much more vocal and better organised in the north-east of the country, there was also a considerable unionist minority in the south. The Tories and Irish unionists literally spoke the same language, describing political differences in Ireland in racial terms, subscribing for the most part to a staunch Protestantism, and drawing upon a shared rhetoric of loyalty and unionism. This support is hardly surprising. While Home Rulers sought to loosen Anglo-Irish ties, unionists desired increasing links, and regarded Ireland as an integral part of the Empire. Even the most moderate of nationalists were portrayed in certain Tory quarters as dangerous rebels, while unionists were presented as a stabilising political force in Ireland. But were unionist (and indeed Tory) fears about the implications of Home Rule actually justified? The bill proposed by Gladstone in April 1886 was actually very limited in its scope, and even then raised strenuous opposition within and beyond his party. Gladstone's intention was to establish an Irish governing body which would sit in Dublin 'to deal with Irish as distinguished from Imperial affairs'; interestingly, he stressed in his speech to the House of Commons the unifying, as opposed to divisive, potential of the bill: 'in such a manner, as would be just to each of the three Kingdoms, equitable with reference to every class of the people of Ireland, conducive to the social order and harmony of that country, and calculated to support and consolidate the unity of the Empire on the combined basis of Imperial authority and mutual attachment.' Gladstone, who spoke for almost three and a half hours, argued persuasively that the Irish were fit for self-government, and that a voluntary secession of power would bind the country closely to Britain without the need for the coercive policies favoured by the Tories. The powers offered to Ireland were therefore clearly circumscribed. Although Dublin would once again be a seat of government, the body established there would have strictly limited powers. Defence and Foreign Affairs would be determined at Westminster, and Dublin would not have control over Irish customs and excise, the principal source of Irish revenue. The Irish Assembly would have certain rights to raise local taxes, but ultimate power would still reside at Westminster, which would in all circumstances have authority over Dublin. Despite its obvious limitations, and intended reassurances for unionist members, the bill was defeated, following the second-reading debate, by 341 votes to 311. Although the margin was not huge, Gladstone had lost several key members of his party over the issue, the most notable being Joseph Chamberlain, who defected to the Tory Party. The issue remained a feature of the British political scene, however, and Gladstone brought a second Home Rule Bill to Parliament in 1893, which was rejected by the House of Lords on 8 September. The defeats did little to dampen Irish enthusiasm for a parliamentary settlement, and indeed the longer it was delayed the greater the faith in Home Rule as an answer to the country's ills grew.

Parnell's increasing determination to secure a constitutional settlement was not accepted by all in Ireland. Land reform remained a
major grievance, despite some significant advances in the early
1880s, and the middle of the decade saw a return to more militant
approaches on the part of tenant farmers. The so-called Plan of
Campaign was first proposed in October 1886 through the pages
of the radical newspaper, *United Ireland*. The work of John
Dillon, William O'Brien and Timothy Harrington, the paper advocated collective action on the part of tenants to strike fair rents,
and proposed that tenants on a particular estate combine to offer
a fair rent to their landlord. If this was refused, they were advised
to withhold any payments, but to put the offered sum into an
'estate fund' which would support them when they were evicted.
Between 1886 and 1890 the plan of campaign took place on 203
estates. The cost of maintaining evicted families was considerable,
but it succeeded both in drawing a good deal of unwelcome attention
to governmental land policy and maintaining awareness of land
issues among the broader population. The plan provoked a two-
pronged approach to Irish affairs from government. The first was
increasingly hard-line as far as violence and illegal activity was concerned. A Criminal Law Amendment Act was passed in 1887 which
allowed the police exceptional powers to repress violent protest,
provisions they were encouraged to use to their utmost extent. The
second was a series of legislative changes designed to address the
defects of land policy, and thereby eliminate grievances at source.
In 1885 the Ashbourne Purchase Act had been passed to encourage
land purchase by willing landlords to their tenants. This was
extended in 1888 by the Land Purchase Act which made considerable additional funds available for the transfer of estate property.
These initiatives, especially the latter, were generally favourably
received by the public, resulting in a brief flowering of the Plan of
Campaign. Hard on the heels of these developments was the vindi-
cation of Parnell in the Special Commission (see above, p. 14),
which concluded in late 1889. By 1890, then, it appeared as though
considerable advances had been made in Irish affairs. Parnell stood
as the undisputed leader of the country, there was a generally good
relationship between the Irish Parliamentary Party and the British
government, long-overdue reforms relating to land-ownership
were underway, and there was considerable hope among nationalists that a Home Rule bill would meet with success at Westminster.

With horrifying speed, the entire political canvas unravelled. Parnell had been having an affair since 1880 with Katherine O'Shea, the wife of an Irish Parliamentary Party colleague. They had had three children, the first of whom was born while he was in Kilmainham Gaol, and although the affair was common knowledge among some of Parnell's closer parliamentary colleagues, it was not widely known. When it became public, through Captain O'Shea's citing of Parnell as co-respondent in the former's divorce petition (O'Shea had known of the affair for years, and lived apart from his wife), many thought that it was another attempt to slander Parnell, and as a result he received a great deal of support. However, when Gladstone denounced the Irish Parliamentary Party leader, and declared privately that he could not work with such an immoral character, the divisions within Parnell's own party grew steadily. In December 1890 it split into pro- and anti-Parnell camps, and plunged into a vicious internal struggle from which it took a decade to recover. Parnell's closest friends advised him to temporarily withdraw from politics to allow the controversy to die down, but he refused. He married Katherine as soon as her divorce decree was made absolute, and continued to campaign for candidates who had supported him, often in the face of considerable hostility. His death in October 1891 was certainly linked to the strain he had undergone in the past few years. It also marked the dashing of Irish hopes as far as Home Rule was concerned, and retarded parliamentary progress in that area until the twentieth century.

As the dramatic events involving Parnell and the Parliamentary Party unfolded, several other developments were taking place in Ireland that would shape political and cultural life in the decades to follow. The period saw the emergence of a disparate series of organisations – literary, sporting, political – which all emphasised Ireland's distinctiveness, and sought to recover elements of a fast disappearing Irish culture. These initiatives are loosely described as the 'Gaelic Revival', or the 'Celtic Revival'. In November 1884 the Gaelic Athletic Association (GAA) was founded by Michael Cusack. Although ostensibly a sporting organisation, the GAA soon adopted a rather more political face. Indeed, many have observed that the entire Gaelic Revival grew to fill the political vacuum caused by the death of Parnell. Although this is not strictly true, it is certainly the case that the decline of the Irish Parliamentary Party, and the absence of any other single political body to replace it, encouraged the growth of organisations which appealed to a broad range of nationalists. The GAA, for example, fostered a strong local sense of identity by establishing sporting competition between counties. However, this emphasis on local pride became much more important when the organisation emphasised the national nature of certain sports, and implemented a ban on the playing of what were designated 'English games' – cricket, hockey and tennis – in favour of Gaelic football and hurling, and by prohibiting any member of the crown forces from joining the Association. The formation of the GAA was only one element within the Gaelic Revival, the intentions of which were many and varied. One was the restoration of the Irish language, another was the encouragement of Irish industries, still another was the creation of a dynamic culture which would forge a new sense of Irish identity, based on a combination of myth and modernity. None of these objectives were in themselves political, but, not surprisingly, many supporters saw the Gaelic Revival as a crucial start to the process of breaking political ties with Britain.

The most important of the various organisations associated with the Gaelic Revival was the Gaelic League. Founded on 31 July 1893, the League's aims were to preserve spoken Irish, restore it as the country's first language, and encourage the revival and creation of literature in Gaelic. The League was explicitly non-political and non-sectarian; indeed the first President was Douglas Hyde, the Protestant son of a Church of Ireland Rector, who taught himself Irish by listening to local people near his home in Frenchpark, Co. Roscommon. The League faced an uphill struggle in its attempt to persuade people of the benefits of learning Irish. By the end of the nineteenth century Irish had gone into lengthy decline, but its loss as a language of everyday use had occurred at an alarmingly swift rate in the nineteenth century. There were several reasons for this. One was the high rate of emigration from Ireland to the English-speaking countries of America, Australia and, of course, Britain. When an expectation of emigration became the norm for young Irishmen and women, the ability to speak English was essential, a process accelerated by the expansion of a national school system from the 1830s which taught only through English. By the end of the nineteenth century, those for whom Irish was a first language were largely confined to the more economically deprived parts of the country, particularly the west, and indeed the speaking of Irish (or the inability to speak English) became increasingly associated

19

with poverty. Thus the Gaelic League had first to make a convincing case for the restoration of the language, and second to find a means through which this could realistically be achieved. Activists were assisted in this by the nationalist separatist movement, which saw the speaking of Irish as a badge of national pride, and a means of distinguishing the Irish from the English. The League grew swiftly in popularity, until by 1908 there were over 600 registered branches. The actual numbers of those who became proficient in the language as a result of League activities are difficult to assess. The fact that many of the leaders of the Gaelic Revival failed to achieve the slightest degree of fluency suggests that they were few. William Butler Yeats, for example, famously never learned more than a couple of words, yet such practical failure made no difference to the fact that he was, and remained, a key figure of the Gaelic Revival, and an exponent of the language movement.

In understanding the Gaelic League and its contribution to Irish politics, one needs to look behind the rhetoric (often irritatingly high-flown and grindingly earnest), and see the organisation as an expression of, and focus for, a range of Irish political and cultural ambitions. For militant separatists, it represented an opportunity to assert an obviously Irish identity against an English one, and its branches offered a nationwide network of fellow activists and potential recruits. For the new Catholic middle class, especially those beneficiaries of second- and third-level education, the League was both a validation of their history and culture, and a sign of their increasing confidence and significance in Irish society. For some Protestant members of the Ascendancy, the Gaelic League, and the Revival itself, presented an opportunity to forge a new identity out of the collapse of the old. Some critics have argued that the Home Rule movement and the assertion of a Gaelic culture allowed Protestant intellectuals the freedom to explore aspects of their culture which had traditionally been ignored because of their association with 'rebel' elements. Some of the most enthusiastic members of the Revival were Protestant, and were either Ascendancy figures or upper-middle class, including Lady Augusta Gregory, W.B. Yeats, Douglas Hyde and John Millington Synge. They, and others, produced an extraordinary body of creative work between 1890 and 1910 which, in addition to drawing upon traditional Irish folklore and legend, also reflected contemporary Irish life, and re-evaluated it in a way never seen before. Synge in particular used the language and expressions of the Aran islanders in his creative works, the most famous (and controversial) of which was his 1907 play, *Playboy of the Western World*. Hyde, less dramatically, published editions of Irish poetry and prose, such as *Beside the Fire* (a collection of folk-tales, 1890), *Love Songs of Connaught* (1893), *Religious Songs of Connaught* (1906), as well as new works of his own in Irish. Yeats drew upon Irish myth and legend in his *Wanderings of Oisin and Other Poems* (1889) and *The Celtic Twilight* (1893). However, Yeats's most emphatically political piece was the play he co-wrote in 1902 with Lady Gregory (although her contribution is frequently overlooked): *Cathleen ni Houlihan*. First performed with Maud Gonne in the lead role, the play explicitly advocated armed rebellion in Ireland's defence, and proved especially popular among nationalists. Although its actual influence has been exaggerated, and Yeats moved a considerable distance from its sentiments within a few years, it nevertheless captured the sense of often-unthinking radicalism in certain quarters of Irish society.

Not all writers active in this period were Revivalists, and not all wrote in praise of a peasant idyll. Sean O'Casey and James Joyce produced works that illustrated a different Ireland, but one which reflected reality for much of the population, especially in Dublin. Neither writer is normally associated with the Revival, but both came to maturity during it, and were influenced, albeit unwillingly, by its emergence. O'Casey was born and raised in the city's slums, a background which made him an enthusiastic, if fractious, supporter of nationalist and socialist reforms. A member of the Irish Citizen Army, he resigned as a result of a clash with Constance Markievicz, which reveals some of the class tensions within the movement. His best work – the Dublin trilogy, consisting of *The Shadow of a Gunman* (1923), *Juno and the Paycock* (1924) and *The Plough and the Stars* (1926) – are plays written in the immediate aftermath of the Anglo-Irish and Civil Wars, and are reflections and critiques of both events. Like Synge, O'Casey used the language of the people in his works, although it was a far cry from the romantic, lilting Hiberno-English of the Aran Islanders. It was the voice of the slum-dwelling Dubliner, albeit exaggerated for comic or dramatic effect, and the settings of his plays were the one-roomed tenement dwellings occupied by so many. O'Casey presented poverty as a grinding rather than purifying experience, and raised the themes of life, death and sex which many preferred to ignore. Dublin was

21

also represented by Joyce, who wrote of the middle and lower-middle classes, mercilessly exposing petty social worlds and criticising the constraints of status and religion he found so suffo-cating. Although he had initially been interested in the Revival, he rapidly tired of what he saw as the futile attempt to invent an image of Ireland which was dependent upon a pastoral innocence which he, among others, questioned had ever existed. Joyce's obsession with Dublin, reflected especially in *Dubliners* (1914), and, most famously, *Ulysses* (1922), provides an interesting counterpoint to much of the literature prompted by the Revival.

In its early years the Gaelic League was associated with a number of other cultural initiatives. In 1891, the Irish Literary Society had been founded in London by Yeats and Hyde, followed by the estab-lishment in Dublin in May 1892 of the National Literary Society. It was here, in November 1892, that Hyde delivered his lecture 'The Necessity for De-Anglicising Ireland', a crucial moment for the Revival, although it has been variously misinterpreted over the years. Partly because of its title, the lecture has been presumed to advocate an elimination of Englishness from Ireland. What Hyde in fact objected to was the vulgarising tendency of certain aspects of English culture, in particular the music-hall, downmarket news-papers and fashion, rather than an incitement to hatred. The lecture was an appeal to Ireland to cultivate precisely that which made it different to England, but which had been voluntarily surrendered. It tied nationality to culture, and implicitly argued that a recognition of Irish difference was the first and most important step towards redefining the Anglo-Irish political relationship:

> It has always been very curious to me, how Irish sentiment sticks in this half-way house – how it continues to apparently hate the English, and at the same time continues to imitate them; how it continues to clamour for recognition as a distinct nationality, and at the same time throws away with both hands what would make it so.

Hyde did not intend that his words should be used for political pur-poses – he always maintained that his concern was to preserve what he feared was a dying culture – but, in the context of increasing dis-cussion of Ireland's future, it inevitably became part of a nationalist discourse.

The debates which raged in the late nineteenth and early twentieth centuries over what might be said to be 'truly' Gaelic, and therefore contribute to the nation's creation of identity, may seem rather facile now. However, they were of tremendous importance to a nationalist movement which sought to legitimise its actions, and, more importantly, argue that it had a separate, distinct (and necessarily superior) history and culture. Moreover, Ireland in this period was slowly modernising. There had been significant improvements in literacy levels, and increasing numbers of the middle classes were entering universities, the importance of which may be gauged by the fact that the majority of the 1916 Rising leaders were well or university educated. Thus nationalists for the most part sought a literature which either appealed as propaganda – *Cathleen ni Houlihan* – or reassured them of their rich cultural heritage, such as the myths and sagas now being incorporated into modern works. They did not especially wish to be reminded of the rural poverty from which they had so recently escaped, nor did they want their movement to be associated with works which questioned their nobility of purpose. However, writers and artists argued that it was not their role to produce rabble-rousing propaganda, or force creativity into the service of politics, and the tension between these two elements was never entirely resolved. As the political mood became more extreme, art and politics were even more closely entwined. In 1915, Douglas Hyde resigned as President of the Gaelic League, declaring that it had become too political and had lost its original purpose as a cultural movement. He actually only formally acknowledged what had long been the case: that an ongoing discussion of Ireland's heritage, and its difference from England's, would link progressively with the campaign for independence.

As part of an increasingly common rhetoric of identity and independence, many Revivalists turned their attention to Ireland's economic potential. Ireland had traditionally been viewed as a predominantly agricultural and technologically backward country, with little industry outside of Dublin and the north-east. However, many were convinced that the country had the potential for significant economic growth, and some further believed that the development of Irish industry would prove the country's capacity for political independence; that Ireland could be made not merely more prosperous, but independent of her largest market, Britain. Arthur Griffith was one who was early convinced of this argument, as were others who did not necessarily share his ultimate political vision. Lady Aberdeen, the wife of the Lord Lieutenant of Ireland, was a tireless champion of Irish products such as Limerick Lace, and did a great deal to promote its products abroad (she also did a tremendous amount to combat tuberculosis in Ireland, but had the misfortune to represent British authority at a time of militant opposition to British rule, with the result that her initiatives met with automatic opposition). It was Sir Horace Plunkett, a Protestant and moderate unionist, who made the most practical advance in promoting Irish industry. In 1889 he launched a cooperative campaign which was intended to address some of the most obvious deficiencies of Irish agriculture. Plunkett wished to encourage regeneration literally from the grass roots, and helped to establish cooperative dairies, and to provide low-interest loans for the improvement of individual and collective holdings. Some initiatives were optimistic in the extreme, such as the plan to turn Ireland into a key tobacco-growing and processing nation, but others proved common-sense strategies to advance the country's economic position. Plunkett also established the United Irishwomen, a progressive movement designed to mobilise female workers, especially agricultural labourers, and became President of the Irish Agricultural Organisation Society in 1894. Much of Plunkett's advice to farmers did not find favour – many were increasing their holdings through the Land Acts, and were not especially interested in cooperative action. Nevertheless, the notion that Ireland was capable of significant economic development remained a key plank in the independence platform, even if this was not proven in practice. Thus, by the turn of the century, many nationalists could look with satisfaction on the various initiatives associated with the Gaelic Revival: if Ireland could support herself economically, prove her cultural distinctiveness through prose, poetry and drama, and find a common ground for individuals from differing religious and political backgrounds to build upon, could political independence be far behind?

CHAPTER TWO

Consolidation and advance, 1900–1914

As Ireland advanced into the twentieth century, an increasing polar-isation of constitutional and radical politics occurred. In many ways it was an extraordinary period as far as political expression was concerned, with parties forming and re-forming constantly, and the emergence of political bodies catering for almost every shade of opinion. One of the most important events however was the refor-mation of the Irish Parliamentary Party (IPP), about to move centre stage in British politics under the new leadership of John Redmond.

Redmond was a Parnellite, and committed to Home Rule. Like Parnell, he recognised the importance of operating on two political fronts simultaneously – the constitutional and the broad-based populist, with the latter's implicit potential for violent action. Where Parnell had assumed the leadership of the IPP and the Land League, Redmond worked actively to ensure that the United Irish League and the IPP became one organisation. The United Irish League, another agrarian protest movement, had been formed in January 1898 by William O'Brien, and within a short period was pressuring government to initiate a system of compulsory purchase of estates in order to ensure rapid land distribution to tenants and labourers. It was wildly successful, attracting 100,000 members in under three years. Although never as explicitly violent as the Land League, it nevertheless, through scale of numbers, proved a formidable body. From the Parliamentary Party's per-spective it represented a significant threat, offering an alternative political body which drew away support from the older organisa-tion. It was this factor which ensured the United Irish League's absorption into the IPP in 1900, with O'Brien's support.

The revitalisation of the Parliamentary Party was influenced by several other factors. The Anglo-Boer War (1899–1902) offered an opportunity for Irish political figures to unite in opposition to Britain as she sought to deny Boer independence. Many Irishmen fought in South Africa on the Boer side, and the progress of the war was watched closely in Ireland, where nationalists saw many parallels between the Boer struggle and their own. As Irish cultural nationalism grew increasingly popular and attracted widespread support, parliamentarians realised that unless the Party resolved its considerable difficulties, its central position might well be usurped by more vital organisations. This is not to say that the rebirth of the IPP was easily achieved. Although it presented a united front, and was most successful in the 1900 general election, winning, along with five independent nationalists, eighty-one seats, Redmond was continually reminded of the potential for discord at the heart of the party. William O'Brien, although actively supporting Redmond's rise as Chairman, remained committed to the United Irish League policy of compulsory land purchase, thereby alienating support from a sector of the population whom Redmond actively courted – Irish landlords. The other key dissenter in the party was T.M. Healy, an anti-Parnellite who had founded the People's Rights Association (another populist organisation which had taken root during the split within the Party) and who acted as a continual thorn in Redmond's side. Both men were to leave the party – Healy in 1900 and O'Brien in 1903 (and to return for varying intervals) – but their presence was a reminder that Redmond could not afford to take the IPP's central political position for granted.

Redmond and the Party pressed hard for Home Rule between 1900 and 1910, with a distinct lack of success. With the Conservatives in power from 1900, hopes for the advancement of the cause were predictably disappointed. Although the Liberal Party, on which Home Rule hopes depended, enjoyed a landslide victory in the 1906 general election, Irish members were to find it a rather different party from that led by Gladstone, and not at all inclined to fulfil that leader's commitment to Home Rule. From the British perspective, Home Rule was an anachronism, a strategy made increasingly redundant by the series of reforms offered since the turn of the century. At the end of the nineteenth century the Congested Districts Board had been created in order to modernise and revitalise impoverished rural areas, principally in the West.

Although not an unalloyed success, it signalled at least an intention to redress Irish grievances. In 1895 Gerald Balfour had been appointed Chief Secretary, and famously declared his intention of 'killing Home Rule with kindness'. In 1896 he initiated a Land Act to improve the distribution of land to tenants, in 1898 he steered the Local Government Act through Parliament, which largely eliminated the traditional local power brokers, the landlords, and in 1899 he established the Department of Agriculture and Technical Instruction, intended as a spur to Irish economic and social development. None of these initiatives entirely fulfilled their respective briefs, but they did indicate the government's willingness to address at least some long-standing Irish demands. This conciliatory policy continued into the twentieth century, with the Wyndham Land Act of 1903 revolutionising land purchase, and starting a process of land distribution that would see 280,000 holdings change hands between 1903 and 1921, and £86 million advanced from the Treasury to finance it.

This not inconsiderable effort and expenditure by the British government made arguments for Home Rule, or at least those based on the necessity for Irish hands to hold the reins of power, less pressing than they had been. In 1907 the Liberals, newly come to power, offered the IPP the Irish Council Bill, a measure that would extend strictly limited controls over certain aspects of Irish administration, principally education, and certain areas of public spending. The bill was reviled in Ireland, although Redmond stopped short of outright condemnation, both because he anticipated the bill's rejection by the House of Lords, and because he feared alienating Liberal support even further. Public reaction however soon convinced him to take a decision, and at the Party's National Convention in May, Redmond rejected the bill emphatically. The Party was in a difficult position however. It was increasingly clear that it depended upon a Liberal Party which was no longer necessarily concerned with delivering Home Rule, while at the same time it was losing political ground in Ireland to new organisations which were not afraid to declare their nationalist agendas.

In defending the IPP's close association with Westminster, Redmond argued that the Party remained passionately committed to Home Rule, but was equally determined to use the House of Commons to secure continued reforms for Ireland in the meantime.

On the surface, this appeared to be a successful strategy. By the election crisis of 1910, the Liberals had undertaken legislative changes which further strengthened local government, improved the transfer of land, and, in 1908, produced a solution to the long-standing difficulty of Irish tertiary education in the Irish Universities Act of that year. But the IPP remained in a vulnerable position, a situation which was to change dramatically with the constitutional crisis provoked by the 1909 budget. The rejection by the House of Lords of Lloyd George's budget led to the dissolution of Parliament, and a general election in which the Liberals won 275 seats and the Conservatives 273, leaving Redmond's men largely holding the balance of power with their seventy-one members. The Party's position was further strengthened by a second election in which the Liberals and Conservatives won 273 seats each, leaving Redmond as the real power broker with seventy-three supporters in the House. Aware that the only way to ensure the passage of a Home Rule Bill was to curb the power of veto held by the House of Lords, Redmond accordingly put the Liberals under pressure to tackle the issue. That party was however already determined to ensure that the House of Lords could no longer block its reforms, and after protracted argument, and under the threat of the mass creation of Liberal peers, the Lords' opposition collapsed. The Parliament Act of 1911 accordingly limited the Lords' absolute veto to a delaying power of two years, and any legislation passed by the House of Commons in three successive years, but rejected by the Lords, would automatically become law. In 1911, then, the Irish Parliamentary Party looked poised to deliver on its promise of Home Rule for Ireland.

But if a week is a long time in politics, ten years is an eternity. While the IPP had steadily pressed its claim with the Liberals, Irish politics had developed, and was to continue to develop, in several different directions. In 1900 Inghinidhe na hÉireann (Daughters of Ireland) was founded by Maud Gonne, the radical nationalist. This women's organisation, formed with the ambitious objective of 'the re-establishment of the complete independence of Ireland', organised a highly successful protest against Queen Victoria's visit to Ireland in April 1900. Since a 'Patriotic Children's Treat' had been planned to honour the Queen, so Inghinidhe na hÉireann organised an alternative nationalist event in Phoenix Park, which was attended by between 25,000 and 30,000 children. The success of the meeting, and the publicity it generated, encouraged a growth in membership, and a broadening of the objectives of the organisation. It encouraged Irish industry through the manufacture and purchase of Irish goods, promoted the Irish language, and began a campaign to provide free school meals for the children of Dublin's slums. Several of the key figures in the organisation, such as Jenny Wyse Power, were veterans of the Ladies' Land League, and they brought a political expertise to the organisation which ensured that it did not become yet another women's philanthropic organisation, but remained focused on political concerns. Inghinidhe na hÉireann proved an important organisation for politically active women, and was to act as a breeding ground for a more radical development.

As the pace of political change in Ireland accelerated, young women became increasingly involved in the various cultural nationalist groups which sprang up throughout the country. When the Irish Volunteers were established in November 1913 (see below, p. 39), women swiftly responded. They formed themselves into a new organisation in April 1914, Cumann na mBan (Council of Irishwomen), which was to play an important role in the subsequent War of Independence. However, their constitution, and their initial activities, suggested that their sphere of influence would be strictly limited. They were created specifically as an auxiliary organisation to the Irish Volunteers, and their aims were 'To advance the cause of Irish liberty; to organise Irishwomen in furtherance of this object; to *assist* [my emphasis] in arming and equipping a body of Irishmen for the defence of Ireland, and to form a fund for these purposes to be called the "Defence of Ireland" fund.' In short, the women were to work in a subordinate capacity, dedicated to the support of the Volunteers. Irish feminists, and in particular individuals such as the feminist nationalist Hanna Sheehy Skeffington, poured scorn on Cumann na mBan for their limited and inferior perception of themselves, but the organisation nevertheless proved very popular. By the autumn of 1914 over sixty branches had been formed, and by 1921 there were an estimated 800, although the number of active members was probably around 3000. Women received a radical introduction to the political process through their involvement in Cumann na mBan, and despite the limits of their constitution, actually participated fully in the Anglo-Irish War, and in the constitutional bodies which accompanied it.

Women were also active in mainstream politics at the beginning of the twentieth century. As in Britain, the question of 'Votes for Women' was a pressing one, and several organisations were formed to secure the women's franchise. But because of the divided nature of Irish politics, some suffrage societies represented only one shade of opinion, such as the Conservative and Unionist Women's Suffrage Association. However, many made efforts to unite on the question of women's rights, regardless of personal politics. The Irish Women's Suffrage Federation was therefore formed in 1911 to unite the various smaller societies, and to campaign together to secure the vote. The suffrage movement in Ireland met with considerable opposition, for various reasons. One was that the body which actually had the capacity to deliver votes for women, the IPP, was decidedly against it. John Redmond was personally opposed to enfranchising women, although even without this antagonism there was a further issue: the IPP had by 1910 a more than reasonable chance of securing a Home Rule Bill, and if Irish suffragists insisted on a clause enfranchising Irishwomen the bill would be rejected by conservatives in the House of Commons, thereby killing what the Parliamentary Party regarded as the greater goal of Home Rule. Among other nationalists, there was a belief that Irishwomen should not legitimise the British government by recognising that it had a right to legislate for them. Still others were concerned that the suffrage campaign would fracture Irish politics, diffusing the energy which should be directed towards the independence movement, and they urged women to offer their support to nationalism rather than suffragism, in the confident expectation that their rights would be granted by an Irish Parliament. Despite these arguments, suffragists feared that if they waited, and withdrew their support for the broader suffrage movement, their rights would be ignored by both British and Irish legislators. It was yet another potentially disruptive element in an increasingly unsettled political environment.

From the beginning of the century, there had been a more political coloration to some of the cultural nationalist groups. In 1900 Cumann na nGaedheal had been founded by Arthur Griffith. The aims of this organisation were not especially radical – to advance independence through a combination of education and economics – but Griffith's personal belief in a form of government based upon the Hungarian example of dual nationality was. To achieve this goal, Griffith proposed that Irish Members of Parliament should abstain from Westminster, and re-establish an Irish Parliament in Dublin. Although Griffith may have over-simplified the Hungarian model, his Hibernicised version proved a powerful personal strategy that fuelled his political activities, while Cumann na nGaedheal was to transform itself into an organisation which would dramatically advance Ireland's progress towards independence. In 1905 one of Griffith's colleagues, Maire Butler, coined the title 'Sinn Féin', meaning 'Ourselves', to embrace a broad spectrum of nationalist activity. In 1907 Cumann na nGaedheal joined with the Dungannon Clubs, a predominantly Ulster-based movement with ideological parallels to the Cumann, and the following year these two joined with the National Council, a broad-based umbrella organisation which attempted to draw together the many small nationalist bodies, to form Sinn Féin. Despite this amalgamation, the membership remained relatively low, and Sinn Féin did not promote an especially radical strategy. Indeed, it was eventually to be propelled centre-stage rather as a result of mistaken identity, when the organisation was wrongly credited with the planning and execution of the 1916 Rising.

Another development was the modest rise of organised labour. By the early twentieth century levels of trade union membership among Dublin workers in particular were very low. This partly reflected the relatively small number of industrial workers in the city, and the very large pool of unskilled unemployed, driven to accept low wages and poor working conditions. Although the situation was somewhat better in Belfast, the centre of north-east industry, sectarian tensions had tended to erode efforts to create a sense of class solidarity, and therefore limited the growth of unions. There had also been long-standing hostility towards unionisation on the part of employers north and south, but especially in Dublin, a situation exacerbated by the fact that a relatively small number of individuals owned or controlled much of the city's business. Foremost among these was William Martin Murphy, who had interests in publishing (as proprietor of the *Independent* newspaper) and business, owning the Imperial Hotel and other significant establishments, and who was vehemently opposed to unionisation. Two charismatic men were to attempt to change the situation – James Connolly and Jim Larkin.

James Connolly was born in Edinburgh, the son of Irish emigrants. Dedicated from an early age to the improvement of workers' conditions, Connolly moved to Dublin with his young family in 1896 to act as the Dublin Socialist Society's organiser. He founded the Irish Socialist Republican Party but attracted few members, facing apathy among the underpaid and underemployed workers, and hostility from politically active nationalists. Although Connolly was himself a nationalist, he was far more concerned with the potential for socialist advance which independence from Britain might bring, rather than independence per se. Connolly dreamed of an Irish Socialist Republic, and proposed a sophisticated structure of nationalisation of public utilities, mass redistribution of property, a welfare state, free education and health care, and universal suffrage. More than any other leader, Connolly understood the appalling conditions suffered by working-class Dubliners, as he lived the same life himself. Nevertheless, his left-wing stance, with its implied criticism of established religion, caused many to view him with suspicion. He also faced opposition from various strands within the nationalist movement, who were either content to allow existing social structures to remain in an independent state – independence being the sole objective – or from those who, even if broadly sympathetic to his reforms, feared that the inclusion of a socialist platform would alienate potential supporters of the independence movement.

The other leader who revitalised Irish labour was James (Jim) Larkin. Like Connolly, this Liverpool-born son of Irish emigrant parents had experienced deprivation at first hand, and was active as a labour organiser in England before his arrival in Belfast in 1907. He was a charismatic leader, although unwilling to consider compromise once set on his course. Enraged by the conditions prevalent in Belfast, and even more so in Dublin, Larkin effectively used the strike against employers, securing some notable victories in his early years. In Dublin in 1908, for example, he secured higher wages for dockers and labourers, and at the end of that year established the Irish Transport and General Workers Union (ITGWU), a body which he hoped would ensure the support of English workers' unions. However, Larkin's undiplomatic persona irritated and alarmed the English bodies, and his belief that the latter should support Irish action through funds and sympathetic strikes was not echoed across the water. He also alienated activists at home, who feared that his attempts to organise the workers would detract from the nationalist campaign, and he especially aggravated individuals such as Griffith, as Larkin's readiness to use the strike as a weapon undermined efforts to establish Ireland's case as a manufacturing success. There were other labour activists who contributed to a sense of change in this period, not least among them Delia Larkin, sister of Jim. She came to Dublin to organise women workers, and met with a significant degree of success, helping to establish the Irish Women Workers' Union. However, her personality was as volatile as her brother's, and she clashed with several co-organisers, as well as falling out spectacularly with Jim Larkin himself. Despite these difficulties with individuals, however, there was an increasing sense that for the first time, workers were becoming more politicised in Ireland, a development viewed with some disquiet by employers.

However, while some significant advances were made, especially with regard to the spread of trade unions, the sheer oversupply of workers, and the low wage structures common in Ireland, made real and permanent change difficult. Labour activity in Dublin in particular seems to suggest that real advances were being made for Irish workers. This is partly the case: in 1911 and 1912 Larkin helped to organise a series of strikes among Dublin dockers which effectively closed the port, and resulted in wage increases. Moreover, trade union membership rose sharply, from 4000 in 1911 to 10,000 by 1913. However, employers were not passively awaiting action on the part of the workers. In 1911, the Employers' Federation had been founded to represent the interests of the business owners, mainly in the city, although it was not until 1913 that the Federation felt itself sufficiently provoked to show its teeth. In August of that year Larkin called out the tramway workers in Dublin, in response to a statement by the Tramway Company that it would not recognise the ITGWU or members of it. Behind this particular industrial action was a long history of tension between Larkin and William Murphy, with each man determined to crush the other. The strike spread rapidly to other components of the Murphy empire, including his publishing interests, but it was the response of the other members of the Federation that turned the confrontation into a crisis. At the end of August, the Federation agreed to lock out any worker who was a member of the ITGWU. This action encouraged other employers to do the same, in a pre-emptive blow against labour organisation, so that an estimated 25,000 men were out of work by September. The leaders on both sides were equally determined to win, but it was the workers and their families, now facing winter with no resources, who bore the brunt.

Initially, support for the strikers was readily forthcoming. British trade union organisations contributed generously to the strike funds (approximately £150,000 in total), and sent over food supplies. Women activists such as Constance Markievicz and Helena Moloney organised soup-kitchens to feed starving families. As usual, it was the children who suffered most, and their appalling conditions led labour activists to propose that some be sent to England to live with sympathetic families until the strike was over. This apparently humane and innocuous action brought down the wrath of the Catholic Church, which declared that Catholic children would be corrupted in English homes. The scheme was abandoned, leaving the unfortunate children to suffer at home. The strike lasted until January 1914, as the employers' willingness to sacrifice short-term profit for what they saw as the long-term advantage of crushing trade union organisation outlasted the workers' ability to go literally without food or housing. Men slowly returned to their jobs (where they still could), and in many instances were forced to agree to a workplace ban on unions. Their experiences left a bitter legacy. The full force of Dublin business interests had been brought to bear against them, and they had endured considerable brutality, especially at the hands of the Dublin Metropolitan Police Force, which had broken up demonstrations and forcibly moved picketers with far more violence than necessary. Partly as a response to this treatment, Connolly, with the professional assistance of J.R. White, a former Army Captain, formed the Irish Citizen Army (ICA), a small band of trained members for the defence of workers' rights. Although never numbering more than 200 individuals, the ICA was an important organisation. It offered equal membership to men and women, and trained both sexes in the use of weapons. It also brought Connolly much closer to the militant republican move-ment, through its implicit condoning of armed defence of rights. Most importantly, it was to prove a vital element in the 1916 Rising, less for the literal contribution to fighting made by members – given their sparsity of numbers – than as a catalyst towards rebellion, once Connolly decided that he would rebel, with or with-out the support of other organisations. And it was Connolly who emerged as the key labour leader after 1913. Larkin, enraged by what he saw as the weakness of English unions in failing to arrange sympathetic strikes, and the apparent victory of the employers, quarrelled with his fellow workers. His absolute commitment to a highly personal vision of labour relations meant that those who disagreed with him were likely to be denounced for weakness, a strategy which did not make for amiable relations. Larkin left Ireland in 1914 to conduct a lecture tour of the United States, and, through a combination of the difficulties of travel during the war and his involvement in American labour politics, did not return until 1923. By that time, the Irish political landscape had changed completely.

The very public tensions expressed in labour agitation had their echoes in more shadowy organisations, which now also geared up for conflict. As far as nationalism was concerned, there were two principal developments which facilitated a move away from constitutional politics. The first was the re-emergence of the secret society, the Irish Republican Brotherhood (IRB), and the second was the creation of the Irish Volunteers (IV), themselves stung into life by the formation of the Ulster Volunteer Force (UVF) in January 1913. The IRB was an oath-bound body formed in 1858, and dedicated to the establishment of an Irish Republic. Also known as Fenians, the IRB was associated with various campaigns throughout the 1870s and 1880s. However, it was a notoriously easy organisation to infiltrate, and, despite some loss of life, had not met with particular success in either achieving independence or persuading the bulk of the country to support it. In 1907, however, Tom Clarke, a veteran Fenian (who had been imprisoned in appalling conditions in England on dynamiting charges in the 1880s), returned to Dublin from America. He set up a tobacconist's shop in Great Britain (now Parnell) Street which was to become the organisational centre for the IRB. Between 1907 and 1912, Clarke nurtured the movement, encouraging young radicals to join, and refining the cell structure (originally adopted to prevent informing, as each cell was independent of each other, but actually leading to widespread confusion) to ensure secrecy. The organisation drew support from men with differing perspectives on the use of militancy, a fact which was to cause some difficulty in 1916. However, all were committed to the goal of Irish independence, even if their opinions on how that should be achieved were diverse. IRB members infiltrated almost all the principal organisations in Ireland before 1914, and were particularly active in the Gaelic Athletic Association and the Gaelic League. The society was denounced by the Catholic Church, but this did not deter many devout Catholics from joining its ranks. Figures for the organisation are unreliable, given its secretive nature, but there were probably around 2000 active members before the First World War, with many more at least affiliated to it. Clarke was the linchpin, but individuals such as Patrick Pearse, Sean MacDermott, and eventually Michael Collins, were to play increasingly important roles, especially following the outbreak of war.

In the years before the Great War, Ireland appeared to be moving steadily towards civil disruption on a large scale. Although avowedly loyal, and determined to resist attempts to weaken the links between Britain and Ireland, it was in fact Ulster unionists who seemed the most likely to provoke violent insurrection on the island. Despite influential supporters at Westminster both in the Commons and the Lords, and the general support of the Conservative Party, Ulster unionists were aware that Home Rule in some form or other was highly likely to be delivered within the next few years. The growing influence of the IPP at Parliament from 1909 made this an inevitability. The unionists therefore decided that the best strategy was to ensure that any Home Rule bill would apply only to the southern counties of Ireland, where Protestants were relatively few in number, leaving the north-eastern corner with its British connection intact. This decision was certainly alarming for southern unionists, who felt that they were being sacrificed by their northern colleagues. There was a good deal of unofficial speculation and even discussion regarding the exact shape of the proposed new body. Should it be the nine counties of the province of Ulster, which had a historic resonance, but would leave an uncomfortably large Catholic population? Should it be just the four predominantly Protestant counties of Antrim, Armagh, Down and Londonderry – politically more stable, but economically weak? Or should it be six counties – the previous four, with Fermanagh and Tyrone, both with substantial Protestant populations? No firm decisions were made, but one thing was increasingly clear: unionists would resist Home Rule, a resistance which would be backed by force if necessary.

The year 1912 saw an escalation of tensions in Ulster. On 28 September, unionists organised 'Ulster Day', on which mass rallies and meetings were held to signal opposition to Home Rule, and during which Ulster's Solemn League and Covenant was signed. This document, based on the Scottish Covenant of 1643, declared

Protestant determination to resist political change. Some signatories were so carried away that they signed in their own blood. Women were not permitted to sign the main declaration, so the female auxiliary organisation to the all-male Ulster Unionist Council, the Ulster Women's Unionist Council, organised a separate petition, which resulted in a greater number of signatures than the male collection (234,046 to 218,206). Like Cumann na mBan, the Ulster Women's Unionist Council was an auxiliary body, bound to assist and support the male organisation rather than formulate policy or act on their own. However, again like Cumann na mBan, the women did a great deal of significant work for which they have only recently received recognition. Because many were the wives of, or related in some way to, key political leaders, they made use of their social contacts to exert pressure on members at Westminster. Women such as Theresa, Marchioness of Londonderry, utilised her considerable social influence to persuade British politicians to support the unionist cause. They were also extremely efficient fund-raisers, and their social status ensured that contributions were substantial. Some individuals were involved in paramilitary activities, although in far fewer numbers than their nationalist counterparts. Some few assisted in the landing and distribution of arms at Larne in April 1914 (see below, p. 38), while others followed the more conventional route of training as ambulance and dispatch riders, ready to assist the UVF. This body was established in January 1913, a date which marked the consolidation of unionist opposition to Home Rule, and introduced the very strong possibility of civil war to Ireland. The UVF, although illegal, grew rapidly and without opposition into a formidable force. Well equipped and trained, with substantial financial support within and outside Ulster, the UVF represented a considerable challenge to constitutional authority by the end of 1913. Unionist leaders drew great comfort from the lack of attempts to suppress the UVF, and in September the Unionist Council leader, Sir Edward Carson, announced that in the event of Home Rule being imposed on Ireland a provisional Ulster government would be established. The implication that this government would be defended by the UVF from any attempts at repression raised the ominous spectre of civil war. Carson was a popular and powerful leader, who retained the loyalty of conservative politicians at Westminster, even as he threatened war in Ireland. An important figure in high political circles, he had represented the government in the prosecution of the Plan of Campaign (although possibly his most notorious case had been the successful prosecution of Oscar Wilde with whom he had attended Trinity College, Dublin), and had taken up the Ulster unionist cause once Home Rule became a certainty. In this he was assisted by Sir James Craig, who was eventually to succeed him as leader.

Official reaction to Carson's declaration was curiously non-committal. It was clear that crisis loomed, a fact confirmed by an unexpected announcement in March 1914. General Hubert Gough of the 3rd Cavalry Brigade stationed at the Curragh Military Camp in County Kildare, and fifty-seven of his seventy officers, declared that, in the event of their being ordered north to enforce Home Rule, they would refuse. This event, popularly known as the 'Curragh Incident' or 'Curragh Mutiny', shook the government out of all proportion to its actual significance (Gough appeared to be under the impression that a march on Ulster was imminent). It did however signal that in the event of armed conflict in Ulster, the government could not necessarily rely upon its own troops, and that if it intended a pre-emptive strike, it might find itself without an army to command. The following month, the UVF in a well-planned manoeuvre landed a large shipment of arms at Larne – significantly, the password chosen for the operation was 'Gough'. UVF troops collected and distributed the weapons, which had come from Germany, throughout the province. It is estimated that 25,000 guns and three million rounds of ammunition were landed; this in addition to the weaponry already held gave the UVF very real resources for armed resistance. From the government's perspective, the danger posed by Ulster unionists was very real. Not only did they publicly declare their intention to resist Home Rule by force, but the loyalty of the crown forces, crucial in the control of civil unrest, could not even be depended upon.

In this atmosphere of heightened tension, yet another organisation emerged. Events in Ulster had been keenly followed by radical nationalists in the south, and the UVF became a source of envy. If unionists could organise efficiently in order to resist Home Rule, then it was felt that nationalists should ready themselves to fight for its implementation. In November 1913, Eoin MacNeill, Gaelic League activist, historian and moderate Home Ruler, published an article entitled 'The North Began' in the League newspaper *An Claidheamh Soluis* (Sword of Light). The article praised unionist action in seizing the political initiative, and urged nationalists to do the same. Although the unionist purpose in forming the UVF was entirely contrary to nationalist aspirations, MacNeill pointed out that their ultimate objective was similar: to forge one's own destiny, and govern oneself. His enthusiastic endorsement found echoes all over Ireland, and resulted in the creation of an organising committee to coordinate efforts. From the outset, this group was dominated by the IRB, which was determined to establish control over what might prove a national force.

Enlistment in fact far exceeded the wildest expectations. After only two weeks of planning, a meeting was held at the Rotunda Rink in Dublin to launch the movement, and attracted almost 4000 recruits. Within six months there were an estimated 75,000 IV all over the country. The leadership, for practical purposes, comprised three men: Eoin MacNeill, The O'Rahilly and Bulmer Hobson, founder of the Dungannon Clubs and member of the IRB Supreme Council. Not surprisingly, there was great anxiety on the part of the IPP with regard to the Volunteers, and a desire to bring it as far as possible under party control. This was resisted by the Volunteer Committee, but it was necessary to disguise overt hostility, as outright opposition to the IPP would risk splitting the Volunteers in two. Redmond insisted in June that Parliamentary Party members be included on the Volunteer Committee, and the Committee was forced to agree. There were therefore two quite antagonistic camps at the head of the Volunteer movement, creating a tension which could not be indefinitely contained. The greatest problem facing the IV however was a chronic lack of arms. Although members drilled enthusiastically with hurleys in place of rifles, or with a small number of antiquated weapons, it was clear they would pose no real threat until they were equipped on the same lines as the UVF. They faced an additional difficulty, though. Shortly after the meeting at the Rotunda, the government had banned the import of arms to Ireland. This diktat had done nothing to hinder the UVF success at Larne, and the IV were determined to pull off a similar coup. The organisation was very poorly funded however, and even supporters in the United States were unable to supply the kind of finance needed to equip a body of the size of the IV.

The necessary funding was to come from a small group of Anglo-Irish nationalists, in particular from Alice Stopford Green, a historian, and Roger Casement, a former diplomat. These two organised the collection of around £1500 (much of which came from their own pockets) in London, and sent Erskine Childers and Darrell Figgis to Germany to buy weapons. It was decided to transport the arms in two private yachts, and one of these, the *Asgard*, manned by Childers, his wife, and Mary Spring Rice, the daughter of Lord Monteagle, landed 1000 rifles and ammunition at Howth, in Co. Dublin on 26 July (another yacht landed at Kilcoole, Co. Wicklow with a further 500 weapons). Seven hundred Volunteers were ready to collect the cargo, and the arms were spirited away to various destinations. It was a great success, not least in publicity terms, but it was to take a violent turn. As news of the landing spread rapidly, there was a euphoric response among nationalists, and, almost predictably, a clash that afternoon between civilians and British troops on Bachelor's Walk, Dublin, which ended with three deaths and thirty-eight wounded (a fourth was to die shortly afterwards of his injuries). There was a huge public outcry. Nationalists pointed out that no effort had been made to prevent the distribution of the weapons at Larne, and in fact there was evidence of involvement on the part of senior British army personnel in the UVF operation. The Bachelor's Walk incident convinced many that in the event of a civil war, which looked increasingly likely, Ulster unionists might have an even greater degree of military support than that represented by the UVF.

Before the situation deteriorated into anarchy, however, the First World War dramatically distracted the attention of many. This was a crucial moment for Ireland. As early as August, Redmond, in a calculated gamble, declared that Ireland would support Britain if she should be drawn into the war. He also proposed that the two Volunteer forces (the UVF and the IV) should be used as a sort of Home Guard, defending domestic security interests. Although this caused a degree of consternation in the ranks of the IV, and indignation among the UVF, who believed that Redmond had no right to make any proposals concerning themselves, it was nothing to the storm which broke on 20 September. On that day, Redmond made a speech at Woodenbridge, Co. Wicklow, in which he appealed to the IV to fight 'not only in Ireland, but wherever the firing line extends, in defence of right, of freedom, and religion in this war'. This unprecedented committal of the IV to the war on Britain's behalf was solely Redmond's initiative, and was made for a number of reasons. The UVF had already pledged to fight, although only after Carson had secured a promise that Ulster would be exempt from any post-war Home Rule settlement. Redmond wished to ensure that nationalists could not be accused of demanding Home Rule without being prepared to assist a neighbouring, friendly state. He also believed that the best way for nationalists to prove that they were worthy of self-rule was to demonstrate that Ireland did not pose a security threat to Britain. Voluntary recruitment would show both a willingness to recognise a common cause with Britain, and place the larger nation under an obligation which would be rewarded with Home Rule. A Home Rule Bill had been placed on the Statute Books, but suspended for the duration of the war. Redmond, like all others in late 1914, did not believe that the war would last for more than a number of months, and his speech was a response to an urgent desire to prove Ireland's good intent towards Britain. It had a more dramatic effect closer to home, however. The IV split into two groups. The majority, numbering around 170,000, followed Redmond, many of them enlisting in the British army. They became known as the National Volunteers. The remainder, around 11,000 men, retained the title of IV, and comprised more radical nationalists, including MacNeill, The O'Rahilly and Hobson, but also men who were to make a dramatic impact in 1916: Patrick Pearse, Thomas MacDonagh and Joseph Plunkett. The IV were dominated by IRB members, and although their numbers were dramatically reduced following the split, those who remained were much more determined upon radical action to secure their aim. The next few years were to turn this determination into action, which changed the political landscape in Ireland for ever.

CHAPTER THREE

The Rising and its aftermath, 1916–1918

The 1916 Rising represents a crucial turning point in modern Irish history, and as a result has attracted a great deal of scholarly attention. However, in many cases historians are divided over what precisely the Rising achieved, and some have argued that it gained its significance less because of its actual military success, and more because of British governmental mismanagement in its aftermath. This is to simplify what was a complex series of events, and a complex series of responses to it. The Rising is important from a variety of perspectives, not least because the Republic was declared during its course, and because it marked a break in Irish politics between constitutionalism and militantism.

The buildup to the Rising was both slow and erratic. Although some nationalists had declared in 1914 that 'England's difficulty is Ireland's opportunity', the First World War was already almost a year old by the time the Irish Republican Brotherhood (IRB) determined upon rebellion, and another ten months passed before decisive action took place. There were several reasons for this delay. The first is that not all the leadership were in favour of armed rebellion, believing that a small rebel force, however keen, would not stand a realistic chance of success against the British army, even with its wartime commitments. The second is that in common with most other observers, the IRB believed that the war would last for months rather than years, thereby limiting scope for action. There was also an initially positive response to the war among many of the population, and, as was noted above, some believed that their participation in the British army would guarantee Home Rule at the war's end. Public opinion was therefore not necessarily behind a violent uprising. As the war dragged on, though, the militant element within the IRB came increasingly to the fore.

Ironically, one of the principal instigators of the Rising was a man who held deep reservations about the form a liberated Ireland should take under nationalists: James Connolly. The slaughter of working-class men at the Front and the potential which revolution contained to reshape society combined to persuade Connolly that an armed uprising represented a real opportunity for change. He was somewhat pessimistic about the possibility of actual military success, but believed, correctly as events transpired, that a symbolic strike against the British in Ireland would mobilise support for independence. In September 1914, Connolly attended a meeting with members of the Supreme Council of the IRB, as well as other interested parties such as Arthur Griffith of Sinn Féin, at which various strategies were discussed. These included coordinating campaigns against conscription, developing links with Germany – by offering support in Ireland for a German invasion in return for assistance in the fight for independence – and executing a Rising during which independence would be declared. This, it was proposed, would allow Ireland to press her claim for separation after the war. Thus from the outset Connolly was aware of IRB plans, however tentative, for rebellion. By 1916, however, he had become disillusioned with the slow progress, and increasingly determined that his tiny Irish Citizen Army (ICA) would stage their own rebellion, regardless of the actions of the IRB and Irish Volunteers (IV). This presented the IRB executive with an immediate and serious problem: if Connolly were to act alone, he would have no chance of success, and draw the wrath of the British government upon Ireland. Up to this point, the government had pursued a relatively low-key policy in the country, in order to minimise support for militant nationalism. A failed rebellion would certainly mean the introduction of coercive measures, and would scupper plans for a larger-scale effort by the IRB. It was therefore decided that a Rising would take place at Easter 1916, which would involve the ICA, the IRB, the IV, and the auxiliary organisations including Cumann na mBan and the Fianna.

The time appeared ripe for such a movement. In May 1915, a military council had been established within the IRB, consisting principally of young men who were in favour of militant action, including Patrick Pearse, Joseph Plunkett and Eamon Ceannt.

In August, Pearse had made a stirring speech at the burial of the veteran Fenian, Jeremiah O'Donovan Rossa, which urged the country towards rebellion. By April 1916 Sean MacDermott, Thomas MacDonagh, James Connolly and the veteran Fenian Tom Clarke had been added to the council, all of whom favoured rebellion. Their plans were kept secret from key individuals such as Eoin Mac-Neill, for although he was supportive of militant action, he had made it clear that it should only be contemplated when a reasonable chance of success existed. Thus although the rebellion was dependent upon the IV, they were to be kept in the dark until the last possible moment. This would allow for a tightly controlled nationwide movement which would maximise success by eliminating the possibility of leaked information by informers within the organisations, the flaw which had condemned previous Irish attempts at rebellion to failure. The military council agreed upon Easter Sunday, 23 April, for the Rising, although Volunteer units were to be told only that they were gathering for a routine march. Within just a few days, however, these plans rapidly unravelled.

In response to negotiations which had begun in 1915, a ship carrying 20,000 rifles, 4 million rounds of ammunition, ten machine-guns and a consignment of explosives left Germany for Ireland to equip a rebellion. Owing to difficulties of communication, the Irish expected the consignment to arrive on Easter Sunday, while the Germans believed themselves expected from the Thursday onwards. The ship, the *Aud*, actually arrived on Thursday, signalling in vain to the shore for an Irish pilot boat to guide her to dock. After successfully evading British patrol ships for almost two days, she was finally captured late on Good Friday, 21 April. The captain scuppered the ship within Cork harbour, literally sinking Irish hopes of a widespread well-armed rebellion. The following day, Sir Roger Casement, returning to Ireland from Germany in order to argue that the Rising should be postponed, was captured on Banna Strand, Co. Kerry. The British had received warnings that a Rising was planned for Easter Sunday, but the under-secretary at Dublin Castle, Sir Matthew Nathan, thought it unlikely. By Saturday, although the arms ship confirmed that a Rising had indeed been planned, Dublin Castle believed they had effectively prevented it. They intended moving against key nationalists as they had originally planned, but thought it unnecessary to act until after the holiday weekend. It was partly the fear of this action which precipitated the IRB's military council into the Rising. However, it was not only the British who read the arrival of Casement and the *Aud* as confirmation that a military engagement was planned. Eoin MacNeill went to Pearse, and was dismayed to discover that the military council intended to press ahead. MacNeill believed that without adequate arms the Rising was doomed to failure, and as leader of the IV, he issued an order to all Volunteer headquarters – which was also published in the newspaper the *Sunday Independent* – cancelling all Volunteer movement on Easter Sunday, thereby countermanding the military council's directive that Volunteer units mobilise at 4 p.m. that day. On Easter Sunday night, the military council issued a further order to the Dublin battalions, the only ones which could be reached in such a short time, directing them to turn out 'for inspection and route march at 10 a.m.' The military council now knew that instead of a country-wide rebellion, the conflict would be centred on Dublin, with far fewer Volunteers to depend upon. Given these circumstances, and the likelihood of failure, its decision to rise has been described as a blood sacrifice, a venture undertaken for solely symbolic reasons. This is not entirely the truth. The leaders hoped that Dublin could be held long enough for Volunteers in the rest of the country to mobilise, and that the British response might be slow, given the army's military commitments at the Front. Although Connolly famously declared on leaving Liberty Hall that the rebels were going to their deaths, this had not been their original intention, which was to fight for Ireland's independence.

The hasty mobilisation was reflected in several tactical mistakes made by the various battalions. St Stephen's Green, the city centre park, was occupied by Michael Mallin and Constance Markievicz's men, despite being almost impossible to defend. Dublin Castle, the centre of the British administration, was attacked, but the rebels abandoned the assault prematurely, believing it to be too well defended to risk losing men. In fact, there was only a skeleton garrison on duty, because most of the troops were on leave for the holiday weekend. A crucial opportunity was therefore lost, and the escape of the Castle allowed the government to easily coordinate its campaign against the insurgents. Rebel headquarters were established in the General Post Office (GPO), and several other strategically significant buildings were occupied, including Boland's Mills, Jacob's biscuit factory, the South Dublin Union, and eventually, the College of Surgeons. City Hall was taken and defended by Dr Kathleen Lynn and Helena Moloney, with support from members of Cumann na mBan. Indeed, this outpost was one of the few where women participated fully in the fighting. For the most part, they were discouraged from taking an active role in combat, although they were allocated more traditional roles such as nursing and feeding the troops. Most famously, Eamon de Valera refused to have any women present at his post in Boland's Mills, a decision he was to regret when he was forced to divert manpower from fighting to catering. But it was the GPO that was to be the scene for perhaps the moment of greatest significance during the Rising: the formal declaration of the Irish Republic. Patrick Pearse read the proclamation to a somewhat bemused audience, announcing not merely the existence of the Republic, but describing the tenets upon which the new state would be laid. Women as well as men were to take their share in society, and the proclamation enshrined democratic principles of government, as well as guaranteeing religious and civil liberty. A provisional government was also declared, and the proclamation was signed on its behalf by Pearse, Connolly, Plunkett, Clarke, MacDermott, MacDonagh and Ceannt. Pearse then returned to the GPO to await the British response.

This was swift in coming. Incensed by this rebellion which they regarded as an act of treason in wartime, no effort was spared to crush it. Because the rebels had failed to take Trinity College, the British had a strongly fortified city centre base from which to launch their attacks, and to severely hamper communication between the rebel outposts. The government also moved troops more rapidly than had been expected, immediately from Belfast and the Curragh, and then within days from England, so that by Tuesday, 25 April, there were over 6500 officers and men in Dublin, and by Friday British troops numbered more than 12,000. Well armed and organised, they pounded the rebel strongholds with artillery brought from Athlone. On Wednesday their fire power was augmented by the gunship *Helga*. Berthed at Sir John Rogerson's Quay on the River Liffey, she destroyed Liberty Hall and bombarded the city. The city was hammered with incendiary and high explosive shells, devastating buildings and causing fires which blazed for days. Before the Rising, Connolly had offered the hope that the British response would be muted, as he claimed that property would be protected above all else. This was proven not to be the case, and buildings, businesses and homes were destroyed with complete abandon. Given their military expertise and their far superior numbers and equipment, the surprising element in the Rising, as F.S.L. Lyons noted, was not that it was suppressed so soon, but that it lasted as long as it did. It is estimated that approximately 1600 Volunteers fought in the city, along with the ICA's full force of 219. There were also the women of Cumann na mBan, many of whom, despite not being officially mobilised, played an important part in communications, nursing and feeding the Volunteers.

The provisional government began the conflict with certain difficulties. Joseph Plunkett had been seriously ill with tuberculosis for some months, and although he was determined to take part in the rebellion, was largely confined to watching the progress of events from a stretcher in the GPO. On Thursday, Connolly was shot in the arm and had his ankle smashed by a ricocheting bullet. Two of the leaders were therefore incapacitated. The rebel posts formed a rough circle in the inner city with the GPO and the Four Courts immediately to the north of the River Liffey, and the South Dublin Union, the Mendicity Institute, St Stephen's Green, City Hall, Jacob's biscuit factory and Boland's Mills to the south of it. The British steadily encircled these positions, and their hold on Dublin Castle, Trinity College, and then possession of the river, allowed them positions of strength from which to bombard the rebels, but also the ability to limit communications between their posts. The rebels also faced another, unexpected, problem. Their chosen headquarters lay close to the inner-city slums, where thousands of Dubliners lived in appalling conditions. When fighting began, and police were withdrawn from their customary posts, many took understandable advantage of the chaos to loot shops in Sackville Street (now O'Connell Street) and the surrounding areas. The rebels were appalled, as they feared that such action would irrevocably tarnish the ideal of the rebellion. They initially acted harshly to deter theft and wanton destruction, shooting some who refused to heed warnings. For impoverished Dubliners however, the confusion of the Rising provided a rare opportunity for material gain, and they continued undeterred.

The looting indirectly caused the most famous civilian casualty of the Rising. Francis Sheehy Skeffington was a pacifist feminist nationalist who abhorred violence and opposed the Rising on the grounds that militantism would inevitably spiral out of all control. When the fighting began, he patrolled the streets, attempting to prevent looting. He was arrested by Captain Bowen-Colthurst, a cousin of the novelist Elizabeth Bowen, and after being held overnight without charge was murdered, along with two journalists who similarly had no connection with the Rebellion. His widow, the feminist nationalist Hanna Sheehy Skeffington, refused all offers of compensation, and finally won an enquiry into her husband's death. Bowen-Colthurst was found guilty but insane, and after a committal of under two years to an asylum was permitted to emigrate to Canada, where he resumed his military career.

Public reaction to the Rising was mixed. In the more affluent areas of the city there was outright condemnation. The destruction of some of Dublin's most handsome streets and buildings was deplored, and the lack of military success, or indeed even the expectation of success, made the action of the rebels appear wildly irresponsible. In working-class areas the response was more mixed. The author James Stephens moved throughout the city during and after the Rising, gathering impressions which were later published under the title *The Insurrection in Dublin* (in November, 1916). He found that there was support in certain quarters, despite the danger in which many civilians found themselves from incidental attack by both British and Rebel troops. This is corroborated by the accounts of many of the rebels themselves, who recounted support from local people in the form of food and shelter. In other sectors there was intense opposition and hostility. One group in particular presented a formidable critique of the rebels. They were the so-called 'separation women' – wives and mothers of men fighting in the British army – and their objections were made on ideological and material grounds. On the occupation of the GPO, the provisional government announced that it was suspending payment of allowances to the relatives of army men. This provoked a furious response, on an obvious level because of the loss of income, but also on a more complex one because the action of the rebels in rising against the British implicitly negated the sacrifices their men were currently making in the First World War. Rebels described how the separation women were prominent among the crowds that jeered them following their defeat. The tensions between these two interest groups would deepen over the next two years.

The response of Irishmen fighting in the British army was also mixed. For loyalists, particularly those Ulster unionists who had enlisted in order to prevent the implementation of Home Rule, the Rising provided confirmation that nationalists were not to be trusted. From their perspective, the rebels were no more than traitors who took unfair advantage of Britain's distraction to launch an attack. In some ways though, this came as little surprise. Before the war, when militantism came to the fore in Ireland with the formation of the Ulster Volunteer Force (UVF) and the Volunteers, political rhetoric had already laid a basis of mutual distrust between unionists and nationalists. The Rising merely provided proof that it would be folly to consider placing Ulster in the hands of such men. In any case, a few short weeks were to provide these men with an even more formative experience, and one which would carry an equally weighty political burden: the Battle of the Somme, which began on 1 July 1916. The Ulster Division, comprised largely of men of the UVF, suffered appalling losses. Because the regiment was largely composed of friends and relatives who had enlisted together, many communities in Ulster lost their young men at one stroke. This trauma led to a hardening of attitudes back home, and gave added urgency to the campaign to exclude Ulster from any Home Rule settlement. It also provided unionists with a symbolic moment to rival that of nationalists. From now on, '1916' would mean two entirely different sets of myths and memories for Irish people.

Far more traumatic an effect was experienced by those men who volunteered for war in the sincere belief that they were fighting to secure Home Rule. For them, the Rising was both a betrayal of their stance and a hint that the sacrifices they were making might be dismissed at the end of the war. No longer content to wait and see if the British government might confer a degree of autonomy on Ireland, the rebels had demanded complete independence. The goal for which Redmond and his National Volunteers strove was no longer enough. This realisation, and the repressive measures introduced by the government after the Rising, had a dramatic effect upon some Irish soldiers, which was only fully realised after 1918. Those men demobilised in Ireland at the war's end entered a changed political environment. Some responded by throwing in their lot with Sinn Féin, and using the deadly skills they had learned in the British army against that same force. For example, Tom Barry, soon to become dominant in the IRA campaign in Co. Cork, was one of those who employed his British army training to Republican benefit, while others kept their heads down, fearful of public hostility because of their army associations. Still others simply disengaged from Ireland entirely. Many demobilised in Britain, returning slowly or not at all as the War of Independence and Civil War progressed. For many men who had volunteered in order to secure Home Rule for Ireland, it proved a bitter blow.

Within a relatively short period of time, the rebel leaders recognised that their campaign, bravely fought as it was throughout the city, was increasingly futile. Whatever slim chance of national uprising had existed on Easter Monday was now beyond possibility, and a continuation of hostilities could only lead to further destruction and death. Pearse therefore decided to offer to negotiate with the British, and sent a nurse, Elizabeth O'Farrell, who had worked in the GPO throughout the Rising, to contact the British commander. On Friday 29 April, she left the GPO under a white flag, and made Pearse's offer to Brigadier Lowe, who refused to treat with Pearse under any terms save that of unconditional surrender, to which Pearse eventually agreed. He himself surrendered to Lowe at 3.30 p.m., and O'Farrell was then assigned the grim task of taking Pearse's order to surrender to the leaders of the other rebel positions.

British government reaction immediately after the Rising was swift and brutal. Convinced that their previous policy of nonintervention had contributed directly to the Rising, they now adopted a heavy-handed approach. Martial law had been declared on 26 April, and a curfew imposed upon the city. Despite warnings that it would alienate moderates in Ireland, martial law was then extended to the whole of the country. The new legislation also suspended the operation of Section 1 of the Defence of the Realm Amendment Act of 1915, and civilians could now be tried by courts martial for a wide variety of offences. It therefore appeared that the government regarded every Irish citizen as potentially rebellious, a suspicion which appeared to be confirmed by the large numbers of arrests made in the days and weeks following the Rising. Thus, although only about 1600 individuals had taken part, nearly 3500 men and eighty women were arrested. Large numbers were gaoled, many in England. One contingent was sent to an internment camp in Wales called Frongoch – this was famously to operate as a university for revolutionaries, where previously moderate types became ardent republicans, and already committed individuals such as Michael Collins created networks for subsequent political action. Although the majority of those interned were released relatively quickly – almost 1300 were out within months, and the majority were home by Christmas – popular opinion had hardened against the government.

It was events at home however which were to have the greatest impact upon political change. General Sir George Maxwell took command of the country, and one of his first acts was to try leaders and participants in the Rising. The trials were held in secret, and the accused had no legal representation and little chance for defence, had they actually believed that their actions required a defence. Ninety were sentenced to death, including Constance Markievicz and Eamon de Valera. Both of these sentences were commuted to life imprisonment, Markievicz on the grounds of sex and de Valera on his American citizenship. In fact, only fifteen executions were carried out, but it appeared to the Irish public as though the process might continue indefinitely. The fifteen executed were Patrick Pearse, William Pearse, Tom Clarke, Thomas MacDonagh, Joseph Plunkett, Edward Daly, Michael O'Hanrahan, John McBride, Eamon Ceannt, Michael Mallin, Con Colbert, Sean Heuston, James Connolly, Sean MacDermott (all in Dublin), and Thomas Kent in Cork. Several of the executions were regarded as particularly brutal, even in the context of the butchery of the First World War. James Connolly was so badly injured that he had to be strapped to a chair to be shot. Joseph Plunkett (dying in any case of TB) married his fiancée, Grace Gifford, in Kilmainham Gaol on the eve of his execution. The deaths were also spaced out over nine days, enough time to allow a feeling of revulsion to grow against the government, and not just among rebel supporters. The parliamentarian John Dillon argued in the House of Commons that the rebels had fought a good fight (a point also made by several British officers) and deserved to be treated more reasonably. The realisation that moderates such as Dillon were outraged caused Asquith to halt the executions. If the government alienated such Irishmen, they would have no means of controlling the country. But the suspension of executions came too late. Martial law remained, and the atmosphere of tension and suspicion was intensified. It became clear that the Irish and the British viewed the situation in entirely contrary ways. From the British perspective, a traitorous rebellion had been legitimately suppressed, and the participants appropriately punished. Moreover, the government feared adverse public response at home if it failed to deal firmly with the situation. The Irish increasingly felt that the Rising represented a game attempt to assert their independence, while the government refused to accept that their actions had any validity. The gulf between citizens and government continued to widen over the next few months.

One of the most important consequences of the Rising however was the political eclipse of the Irish Parliamentary Party (IPP) by Sinn Féin. As one of the largest nationalist organisations in the country, it was wrongly assumed that it, and its leader Arthur Griffith, had been behind the rebellion. Indeed, the events of Easter week were commonly referred to as the Sinn Féin rebellion. This was far from the truth, yet the imprisonment of large numbers of Sinn Féin members immediately after the Rising both hardened attitudes within the organisation, and had the effect of causing large numbers to join it as a sort of protest. Within eighteen months of the Rising police estimates put the number of Sinn Féin members (or Shinners as they were disparagingly termed) at around 250,000. Although the bloody events of Easter week had given Sinn Féin its initial boost, by 1917 its leaders were formulating a political agenda which was not dependent upon violence. This reassured many who had previously been IPP supporters, thereby alienating large numbers from the party. Presiding over this growth were the newly politicised ex-prisoners, who came to hold increasing sway over the organisation. The first indication of the direction the winds of change were blowing came in January 1917. A by-election was held in North Roscommon, which the IPP candidate was expected to easily win. Sinn Féin however persuaded Count George Noble Plunkett, father of Joseph Plunkett, to stand as an independent, but with their clear backing. He won the seat easily, providing the first example of how an association with the men of 1916 could reap dividends. On Sinn Féin advice, Plunkett announced that he would not take his Westminster seat, setting the separatist tone which would characterise Sinn Féin policy for the next four years. In May, the IPP lost another safe seat, in Longford, to Sinn Féin. However, the most significant demonstration of change, and a herald of things to come, was the election of Eamon de Valera in the East Clare by-election of July 1917. His campaign was fought on an explicit association with 1916, both as one of the few surviving leaders of Easter week, but also as one who affirmed the independent republican ideal declared at that moment. It was the start of a lengthy and eventful political career. By the time of the Sinn Féin Ard-Fheis (annual convention) in October 1917 the released prisoners, and the now radical Sinn Féin party, were in the political ascendant. Thanks to the selflessness of Arthur Griffith, who stood aside, de Valera was elected President of Sinn Féin, and was also elected President of the Volunteers. The Ard-Fheis was notable for a resolution proposed by de Valera, that 'Sinn Féin aims at receiving international recognition of Ireland as an independent Irish Republic. Having achieved that status the Irish people may by referendum freely choose their own form of government.' This was a remarkably liberal statement, given the context of revolutionary chaos in which the new Sinn Féin had been conceived, but it was in line with the democratic principles out-lined in the 1916 Proclamation. It also signalled an intention to push the political agenda beyond the traditional Anglo-Irish forum.

The IPP on the other hand slid into a startling decline. This may be attributed to several factors. The first was that after 1916 the Party became associated with an obsolete political goal, that of Home Rule. The majority of the country now called for an independent republic, even if few could comfortably define what that might mean. Through no fault of its own, then, the Party was left with an outdated agenda, and the more radical political position had already been taken by Sinn Féin. Second, by continuing to hold seats at Westminster, the IPP remained an integral part of the British political establishment. Its argument that change and progress could be more swiftly secured by working within the system fell on deaf ears, and its nationalist credentials were undermined by its continued association with British parliamentarianism. Third, a significant percentage of traditional IPP supporters switched their allegiance to Sinn Féin, because of their newly respectable political programme. Finally, in March 1918 John Redmond died, and although Dillon was a more than adequate leader, the party had lost a key figurehead. In April, the British government raised the possibility of introducing conscription to Ireland, and Dillon with-drew his party from Westminster in protest. Even this dramatic move was not enough to save the party, and the elections of 1918 saw numbers decimated.

After the 1916 Rising, the British government became increasingly worried about the state of the country, and the efforts which might be required to control it. There was growing pressure from the

United States to resolve the crisis, and America's recent entry into the war made this demand all the more urgent. In May 1917 Lloyd George therefore proposed to Redmond that Home Rule be immediately granted to twenty-six counties, and the most intractable six north-eastern counties excluded. Redmond flatly refused. This sort of settlement was anathema to everything he had fought for, and he correctly foresaw the potential dangers of partitioning a small country like Ireland. Lloyd George then proposed that an Irish Convention be held, in order to allow the representatives of each of the main political groupings in the country to resolve their differences. The convention was a last-ditch attempt to secure accommodation between the different interest groups in Ireland, and represents an effort by Lloyd George to distance the British government from the 'Irish Question'. The idea was that the Irish themselves, republicans and unionists, Catholic and Protestant, would determine the country's future. A good idea in theory, it proved impossible to organise in practice. The war and the Rising had placed interest groups in positions far removed from each other, and each felt that they had made sacrifices which could be rewarded only by the full implementation of their rights. The only participants who greeted the convention with enthusiasm were those who were in fact facing political bankruptcy. Thus the IPP and the Southern Unionists made efforts to ensure its success, while it was boycotted by Sinn Féin and organised labour, and observed, but not encouraged, by Ulster unionists. The country appeared to be growing increasingly polarised, a development all the more worrying now that armed rebellion had been established as a precedent. To this volatile situation another potentially explosive element was added: conscription.

From early 1916, the question of conscription had been raised in British political circles. The heavy losses sustained by Britain in the war, and especially at the Battle of the Somme, where so many Irishmen died, led a substantial proportion of the population to believe that imposing conscription on Ireland was a necessary step. There was also considerable resentment that nationalists had staged a Rising when Britain was preoccupied in Europe: the forcible enlistment of these men, it was felt, would have been a practical deterrent against rebellion. But any suggestion that Irishmen should be coerced into fighting in the British army met with strong opposition. Redmond was wholeheartedly against conscription, because he believed that Ireland would make the most emphatic statement regarding her capacity for self-government, and her trustworthiness as a pacific neighbour, through voluntary enlistment. More extreme nationalists absolutely refused to consider that Britain had any right to Irish support for the war, regarding the conflict in Europe as a struggle between imperial powers that had nothing to do with Ireland. Irish unionists, north and south, tended to hold the opposite view, although there were some contradictory currents of thought. For the most part, they believed that, as an integral part of the United Kingdom, Ireland had an obligation to play her part in the war, and felt that she exposed herself to charges of cowardice by avoiding this responsibility. Some northern unionists however hoped that their voluntary enlistment, in contrast to nationalist refusal, would result in special consideration at the war's end. Conscription would muddy the waters significantly, and make special pleading more difficult.

As far as the British government was concerned, conscription for Ireland was an extremely delicate issue. Despite its imposition on the rest of the United Kingdom in 1916, Ireland had been exempt. However, early 1918 saw the British government in a state of extreme anxiety with regard to troop numbers. Heavy losses, especially in the first two years of war, had created a shortage which looked set to become acute. The imposition of conscription on the country would provide both fresh troops for the war, and appease unionists in Ireland and Britain, by forcing Irishmen to participate on Britain's behalf. The clear difficulty lay in the likelihood that conscription would precipitate rebellion, placing the government in the position of fighting a war on two fronts. Lloyd George decided to test the water through an enabling bill, and on 10 April proposed the Military Service Bill. This measure did not enact conscription, but empowered the government to extend it to Ireland should it become necessary. The suggestion proved enough for Ireland. The leader of the IPP, John Dillon, who had taken over on Redmond's death on 6 March 1918, withdrew from the House of Commons in protest, and joined Sinn Féin in the Mansion House on 18 April to pledge their opposition to conscription. All over the country, people signed a petition outside churches which read: 'Denying the right of the British government to enforce compulsory service in this country, we pledge ourselves solemnly to one another to resist conscription by the most effective means at our disposal.' The 'most effective means' certainly implied armed resistance, something the government clearly wished to avoid. Yet the possibility of actually losing the war was a much greater threat than a rebellion in Ireland, and even a nationwide strike by the Irish Trades Union Congress on 23 April did not eliminate the threat of compulsory enlistment. Lloyd George stayed his hand for a time, although he did attempt to ready the government for conflict in Ireland should he believe that conscription needed to be imposed. He appointed Lord French as Lord Lieutenant in May, hoping that a seasoned military campaigner would ensure the success of conscription. French was given considerable powers, which he first used on 17 May, when the majority of Sinn Féin and Volunteer leaders, apart from Michael Collins and Cathal Brugha, were arrested. The government claimed that there was evidence of a 'German Plot' – an alleged attempt by republicans to use Ireland as a base for German attacks on Britain – but it was in fact a simple governmental strategy to remove from circulation those men who were most likely to lead Irish opposition to conscription. In fact, the initiative backfired badly, with a sharp increase in support for Sinn Féin which had its clearest expression in the election of the imprisoned Arthur Griffith for East Cavan in June (see below, p. 58). The physical removal of individuals was clearly not enough to disrupt Irish opposition, and the government faced serious conflict if it attempted more radical action. As the year advanced, attitudes on both sides hardened. The explosive situation was dampened only at the end of the war, when conscription became an irrelevance.

The end of the First World War heralded a new era in Anglo-Irish relations. In the general election of December 1918, Sinn Féin won a remarkable victory, claiming seventy-three seats. The Parliamentary Party won only six, a definitive statement of its decline. Electoral reforms had significantly increased the number of eligible voters, especially the young, and large numbers of women. These individuals appear to have voted mainly for Sinn Féin, a fact that caused some disquiet in political circles. Ireland now seemed to be dominated by young, idealistic radicals, who had come to political maturity in a context of militantism. This would have significant consequences over the next five years.

CHAPTER FOUR

The Anglo-Irish War, January 1919 to July 1921

The Anglo-Irish War, also known as the War of Independence, began on 21 January 1919, and ended in a truce on 9 July 1921. This short period marked great changes for the country, in which forces of democracy and revolution progressed hand in hand. The campaign for independence was conducted on two fronts. The first was the establishment of a de facto republic, with its own judicial and administrative system, which operated entirely independently of British administered rule. The second was a military campaign, conducted by the newly formed Irish Republican Army, which harried and harassed the crown forces throughout the country. In many cases, the same individuals were active in both arenas. This chapter will examine these two developments, and their interdependence, up to the truce of 1921.

The end of the First World War was greeted with general relief. Aside from the obvious benefits of the cessation of violence, ordinary people could now look forward to political change. The suffrage campaign, so hard fought before the war, was finally about to bear fruit. On 6 February, the electorate had been significantly enlarged through the enfranchisement in Ireland of all men over the age of 21 and most women over age 30. Thus those eligible to vote grew from over 700,000 in 1910 to almost two million in 1918. The general election of 14 December was the first opportunity for these new voters, who were for the most part nationalist in their politics, to express their opinions. The results were certainly dramatic. Sinn Féin swept the board, increasing its seats to seventy-three from seven. Unionist strength increased by eight to twenty-six. There were no Labour members, their having agreed with Sinn Féin not to run candidates in order to prevent splitting the vote. Long term, this was to prove a poor tactical decision on labour's part, and there was no significant labour representation in the Irish parliament for many years. The most startling change in 1918 however was the decline of the Irish Parliamentary Party. From its pre-war dominance as the soul of Irish nationalism, it was reduced to a paltry six seats. The result was shocking, but not entirely unprecedented. From their relatively harmonious relationship during the anti-conscription campaign, relations between Sinn Féin and the Irish Parliamentary Party had deteriorated badly. The crisis had come during the by-election at East Cavan in May 1918. Despite having agreed in other cases not to run opposing candidates, Sinn Féin decided to propose Arthur Griffith for the seat. Griffith had always been critical of Irish Parliamentary Party policy, but it was the fact that, immediately before the election, the government made the tactical error of attempting to round up the key Sinn Féin leaders, an action which both alienated public opinion and engendered more support for Sinn Féin. The government did indeed succeed in arresting many activists (Michael Collins and Cathal Brugha managed to evade capture), and Griffith among others duly went to gaol. It turned out however to be a propaganda coup for Sinn Féin. From prison, with the help of a clever Sinn Féin campaign which played upon his detention, he was elected with a large majority. The experience was a valuable one for Sinn Féin, which was now confident that it could successfully challenge the Irish Parliamentary Party and, with the assistance granted by heavy-handed government from Britain, ensure public sympathy for its campaign. It was a lesson which was put to good effect during the general election, in which thirty-four prisoners were elected to Westminster. These included Constance Markievicz, the first woman to be elected to the House of Commons.

In line with the stance taken by Count George Noble Plunkett in 1917, the newly elected MPs declared that they would abstain from Westminster. Instead, they called a meeting of a separate Irish Parliament, which met for the first time on 21 January. Known as Dáil Éireann (the Assembly of Ireland), it was to be composed of all the newly elected Irish members, but both the Unionist and Irish Parliamentary Party members refused to attend, leaving it an exclusively Sinn Féin gathering. It met in the Mansion House in Dublin and, although the members sat for only two hours, decisions were made which were to have a significant bearing on subsequent political developments. In a statement read to the Dáil – the Declaration of Independence – the proclamation of the Irish Republic made during Easter week in 1916 was confirmed, and the Dáil pledged to securing it. In mid-1919 an oath of allegiance to the Republic was taken. This commitment was to be the cause of unimaginable hardship after 1921, when the Dáil divided over whether the Treaty could be accepted without the bestowal of a republic. In 1919, however, few gave much thought to whether they were creating an ideological noose, and gladly endorsed the republican ideal. The declaration also confirmed the democratic principles of the 1916 proclamation, and affirmed the rights of Irish citizens to equality and freedom. These liberal principles were further underlined in the Democratic Programme, a paper which was presented to the Dáil and approved on the same day. This document, with a strong labour emphasis, declared that 'all right to private property must be subordinated to the public right and welfare', a radical statement by any standards, and one which implied that all citizens should have a fair share in the country's resources in return for their work. The Democratic Programme ensured that although there was no direct labour representation in the Dáil, labour, and even socialist, principles were declared. However, the generosity of these ideals was rather overtaken by subsequent political developments, and several fell by the wayside in the early years of what was to become the Free State.

The second meeting of the Dáil, held on 1 April, was rather better attended. The government had released most prisoners (de Valera had escaped from Lincoln Gaol in February, with Collins' help), so the Assembly was able to proceed with the task of establishing a government. Eight ministers were appointed: Michael Collins (Finance), Constance Markievicz (Labour), Arthur Griffith (Home Affairs, and Deputy to the President), Cathal Brugha (Defence), Eoin MacNeill (Industry), Robert Barton (Agriculture), George Noble Plunkett (Foreign Affairs), and W.T. Cosgrave (Local Government). Eamon de Valera became President of the Dáil. Although the titles may have accorded a certain respectability, the majority of the members, and especially the ministers, were the focus of interest for the British government. As a result, the Dáil met infrequently and in secret, and often without key individuals. Despite its unusual circumstances – for example, there was no opposition party – the Dáil functioned as far as was possible as a properly constructed parliamentary body, observing protocol and procedure. The willingness of the general population to support the Dáil, despite its unofficial status, may be seen in the success of the 'Dáil Éireann National Loan'. This initiative, launched by the tireless Michael Collins, raised over a quarter of a million pounds at home and abroad. The determination to form a real government was also reflected in administrative developments outside of the Assembly.

From early 1919 until the end of 1920 Sinn Féin expended a great deal of energy in ensuring that they secured power at local as well as high political levels. In January and June 1920 local elections were held throughout the country. Sinn Féin repeated the success of the general election, gaining control of seventy-two out of 127 corporations and town councils, and sharing power with other nationalists in a further twenty-six. Its power at county-council level was almost total, as it held twenty-eight out of thirty-three, and controlled 138 out of 154 Poor Law Boards. This gave it the authority to break with the existing Local Government Board, and to operate a separate system of local government in opposition to the British, an initiative which began early in 1919, but which was officially sanctioned in June of that year. Such an extraordinary development could only succeed with the support of the mass of citizens who participated in it, and nowhere can their approval be more clearly seen than in the so-called 'Dáil Courts' – the alternative judiciary which began operations in 1919. Originally begun as 'arbitration courts', established to deal principally with disputes over land-ownership and rental, the courts rapidly spread from West Clare to the remainder of the country, with the exception of the north-east. The courts proved so popular that it was necessary both to create additional forces to implement their decrees, but also to formally establish a tiered legal system, based upon the existing British model. Thus a republican police force was formed, and a special land court created to handle the huge numbers of disputes. In September 1919 a system of four levels of administration was formally created. This consisted of Parish Courts, which dealt with relatively minor issues; District Courts, which handled appeals from the Parish Courts, as well as more serious criminal cases; District Courts in Special Session, which sat three times a year, presided over by a Circuit Judge, of whom four were appointed; and finally the Supreme Court, sitting in Dublin. With some minor modifications, British law and legal practice prevailed in the courts. When the courts began to operate, there were understandable fears that they would favour appellants who declared themselves to be republicans, or that old scores would be settled against, for example, Protestant or unionist landowners. In fact, perhaps because of a determination to prove their capacity for fair government, the courts were recognised by even hostile observers to be generally moderate and just. Their success was all the more remarkable since many of those appointed had little or no legal training. They moreover provided an opportunity for women in particular to participate in this judicial revolution. Participants remembered that they applied as far as possible simple common sense to the cases before them, and that most were reasonably happy with their judgments. What the courts and the new system of local government achieved, then, was to make British rule, at a judicial level, unenforceable. People simply took their cases to the republicans, and although the legally appointed, British, system remained in existence, it ceased to have credibility.

The civilian population contributed to the nationalist cause in other ways. In May, railway workers protested against the transport of munitions by refusing to handle such goods. This protest was soon extended to armed troops themselves, so that drivers would refuse to move trains on which soldiers travelled. Despite threats of unemployment, and frequent clashes with the soldiers themselves, this boycott was maintained. Although the numbers of soldiers actually inconvenienced were relatively few – it was increasingly unsafe for troops to travel on civilian transport in any case – it was symbolically important. The strike was called off in December 1920, and only then because the government had threatened to close the railway system in retaliation.

The British government naturally refused to acknowledge the validity of bodies such as the Dáil courts, or to be intimidated by the railway strike, and continued to govern the country through a combination of coercion and decree. From the outset, however, the pace was set by the Irish. By coincidence, on the same day that the Dáil met for the first time (21 January 1919), the military campaign also began. In Soloheadbeg in Co. Tipperary, three Volunteers (Dan Breen, Sean Tracy and Seamus Robinson) ambushed a party transporting explosives to a local quarry, which was being escorted by the Royal Irish Constabulary (RIC). Two policemen were killed, and the explosives seized. Although it was not conceived as such, the attack marked the beginning of a concerted campaign against the

RIC by republicans which was to have a devastating effect. Despite the fact that the police force was drawn from the local community, a campaign of boycott was initiated, and RIC men and their families were subject to intimidation and abuse. As an armed force, they were also the best source of weaponry for militant republicans, who were desperately short of arms and ammunition. RIC barracks therefore became prime targets for attack, both in an attempt to force the occupants to abandon any attempts to enforce the rule of law, and to secure weapons.

Within a relatively short period of time, and in response to the rapidly changing political environment, the Volunteers underwent a transformation. Under Cathal Brugha as Minister of Defence, the Volunteers were brought under the control of the Dáil. Brugha did this by having the Dáil agree that the Volunteers should also take the Oath of Allegiance along with Dáil members. Although this proved impossible to implement *en masse*, the principle was accepted, and the Volunteers therefore became the effective army of the Republic. Their official title was Óglaigh na hÉireann, but they became known as the Irish Republican Army (IRA). However, although Brugha was theoretically in control of the IRA in his ministerial capacity, the reality was far more complex and unsatisfactory, for the following reason.

As the Dáil established and approved the initiatives which created an oppositional government in Ireland, the military campaign continued apace. Some individuals were actively involved in both camps, none more so than Michael Collins. In addition to his governmental responsibilities, Collins was also Director of Organisation and Director of Intelligence, and was therefore at the heart of the IRA campaign. In addition, he remained a member of the Supreme Council of the Irish Republican Brotherhood (he would eventually become President), an organisation viewed with intense hostility by both Cathal Brugha and Eamon de Valera. As poachers turned gamekeepers, they knew the potential for disruption which the IRB still held, and pointedly refused to countenance any action on its part. They had in fact implicitly criticised the entire organisation through their refusal to rejoin it after 1916. Although relations were ostensibly cordial between all three men, there was growing tension over Collins's roles, and the importance he assumed within the independence movement. For Brugha, antagonism centred on the fact that Collins appeared to lead the IRA campaign, while

Brugha was nominally in charge. This is not to underestimate Brugha's importance – he was a formidable and uncompromising individual, who commanded a great deal of respect from his men – but Collins both inspired an extraordinary degree of loyalty from his followers and was an intensely secretive organiser. Well aware that previous Irish clashes with the British had failed because of infiltration by informers, Collins developed a sophisticated network of activists who took their orders directly from himself, and who were often unaware of the identity of their fellow workers. This system worked with an extraordinary degree of efficiency, but it had the unfortunate effect of engendering suspicion in the minds of people like Brugha, who felt undermined by Collins' individualistic campaign. With de Valera the relationship was more complex. The two men were to emerge as the most important figures in the independence movement, but for different reasons. De Valera was the iconic 1916 veteran, whose apparently transparent statements on the Irish situation masked a convoluted, and ruthless, approach to power. By April 1919 he occupied several key positions – Priomh-Aire (President) of the Dáil, President of Sinn Féin, and President of the Volunteers. Collins, however, exercised direct control over much of the military campaign, as well as playing a central role in the administration of the Dáil, and was a popular and charismatic leader. A Post Office clerk who returned from England to take part in the Rising, he matured swiftly into a brilliant military tactician, and a formidable political thinker. He was also, however, a pragmatist, and his realistic assessment of what was achievable by the Irish was to clash fatally with Brugha and de Valera's idealistic conception of what the struggle was capable of achieving.

The war of independence was a guerrilla campaign, fought with varying intensity in different parts of the country, and conducted in a series of different phases. Levels of commitment were heavily dependent upon the enthusiasm of individual leaders, and as the campaign progressed, several figures were to emerge as the key players, both in this war, and in the civil war which followed. Within a short period of time, there emerged a series of flying columns – small bands of men who struck at the crown forces, and disappeared back into the countryside, merging with the general population. This profile, although highly effective in terms of harassing the British forces, brought civilians into the heart of the conflict, as they came under constant suspicion of supporting the flying columns and were accordingly punished. The war is commonly described as falling into three main phases. The first was relatively low-key, and lasted from early 1919 to early 1920. This period was principally taken up with attacks upon police barracks and the police themselves, and was part of the campaign to arm the IRA. The RIC was at this stage the main source of weapons for the ill-equipped IRA – the attack at Soloheadbeg may be explained not as an attack upon the crown forces per se, but an attempt to secure arms and explosives – and were therefore a logical target. The second phase of the war represented the most direct engagement by both sides with each other, and saw the conflict escalate alarmingly. This lasted from the first months of 1920 through to the end of the year, culminating in the bloodiest of attacks by both sides. The final phase began at the start of 1921 and, although marked by the implementation of an official government policy of reprisal, it saw the war settle into a series of guerrilla attacks by flying columns, and end with the truce in July.

The first phase of the war was one in which both sides sought to consolidate their positions, testing new strategies, and the capacity of the other to deal with attack and counter-attack. One of the most striking developments was the ruthless efficiency with which Michael Collins and his small army of agents dealt with key British intelligence figures, and those officials charged with uncovering and confiscating Sinn Féin funds. These were considerable: in April, the Dáil had approved the issue of Republican Bonds to the value of £250,000, and Collins as Minister for Finance was responsible for this (in 1919) vast sum. Furthermore, there were considerable monies being raised for the cause outside of Ireland, especially in America. De Valera left Ireland in June for the United States, to secure American support for the Republic and to raise funds. He was away for eighteen months, a fact which appears to have contributed to certain difficulties in his relationship with Collins after 1920. While in America, he became embroiled in existing tensions between the two main leaders of the Friends of Irish Freedom, John Devoy and Judge Daniel Cohalan. Despite de Valera's rank as President of the Dáil, they were not especially deferential to him, or willing to accept his plans for the future of the country. He did however succeed in raising huge amounts of money: $5 million in total from an Irish bond drive. Some of the money was retained in America for use in promoting Ireland's cause, but the bulk of it, around $4 million, was sent home. Collins squirrelled this money away from the British authorities, adopting an elaborate system of accounts and fronts to conceal its origin and use. The necessity to keep at least half a step ahead of the British authorities led Collins to persuade employees throughout the British administration in Dublin to pass useful information to him. This meant that he was able to identify spies and informers, as well as keeping well informed regarding British security plans. He made intelligence officers his particular target: many detectives of the 'G' division of the Dublin Metropolitan Police were assassinated, and attacks upon police throughout the country were common. At the end of the year, an unsuccessful attempt was made on the life of the Viceroy, Lord French. In one of the many ironies of the conflict, Lord French's sister, Charlotte Despard, was also in Ireland, working with Maud Gonne for the Irish nationalist cause, and making use of her brother's name to ensure safe passage through army and police checkpoints. Throughout this period, the Dáil courts continued to operate, leaving the British government in something of a quandary with regard to how to tackle the various strands of Irish activity. This indecision is reflected in the fact that clearly identifiable organisations were permitted to operate until late 1919. Although Sinn Féin, Cumann na mBan, the Gaelic League and the Irish Volunteers had been proclaimed illegal in Co. Tipperary in early July, it was not until September that they were so declared in Cork, and throughout the whole country in November. Most surprising was the delay in proscribing the Dáil – it did not officially become illegal until September 1919.

Nineteen-twenty proved the worst year of the war. Although the Dáil continued to operate as an underground institution, and the Republican courts dispensed justice almost uninterrupted, military engagements became more frequent and intense. The RIC as a force became less significant, both as a result of continued attacks and diminished numbers through resignation and a drop in recruitment. Although the murder of the two policemen in Soloheadbeg had been committed without any sanction, on 31 January 1919 Cathal Brugha issued a directive to the Volunteers, stating that all soldiers and policemen of the crown were to be regarded as legitimate targets. The RIC was therefore the principal focus, as it was expected to continue to operate within communities, unlike soldiers who were confined to barracks for much of the time. Not surprisingly, between the campaign of boycott and the threat of murder, numbers of RIC members fell dramatically. These men and their families had been placed in extremely difficult positions – they lived locally, were well known to the Volunteers, and were extremely vulnerable not merely to physical attack, but also to intimidation and boycott by their neighbours. It was little surprise therefore that many resigned or moved to escape unwanted attention. In casting about for means to augment the police force, and with chances of recruitment low in Ireland, the government made a decision which was to create one of the most notorious forces in the country: the Black and Tans.

These troops were recruited as an emergency response to the deteriorating policing conditions in the country. Officially merely a reinforcement of the RIC, not a replacement, the new recruits acquired their nickname because of the mixed uniform the first men wore – khaki army uniforms teamed with dark green police caps and belts – because of lack of time to equip them properly. The colours echoed that of a famous pack of hounds in southern Ireland, and it was a name which stuck. It is often said that the Black and Tans were recruited from gaols in England, and offered a remission of their sentences in return for service in Ireland. While this is untrue, the ferocious reputation these men rapidly acquired, and the difficulty their commanding officers had in keeping control over them, contributed to the impression that the security situation in Ireland was almost entirely out of control. The Black and Tans were for the most part ex-army men, many of whom had been unemployed since demobilisation, and who experienced difficulty in adjusting to civilian life. A large number were still coming to terms with their experiences in the First World War, a fact which may partly explain, if it does not excuse, their reckless and aggressive behaviour in Ireland. The environment in which they now operated was very different from their previous experiences. The Anglo-Irish War was conducted on guerrilla lines, with no clear lines of engagement. Troops were attacked, while their assailants simply merged with the civilian population. Patrols were ambushed, sniping was common, and the Black and Tans, never the most disciplined of forces, responded to this strain with intimidation and pre-emptive violence. In June, another force was created to assist in policing Ireland – the Auxiliary Division. The Auxiliaries were drawn from the officer class of the British army, and were, like many of the Black and Tans, men who had fought in the First World War.

They too were regarded with fear and distrust by the Irish, and swiftly acquired a reputation which equalled that of the Tans. Both of these forces were exceptionally well paid – the Auxiliaries received £1, and the Black and Tans 10s. per day, a rate of pay unheard of at this period, a reflection of the difficulty in recruitment which the British government faced, and the very real danger posed by the Anglo-Irish War.

Estimates of the total number of troops in Ireland vary, but what is clear is that within a relatively short period of time the country was geared up for war, while, at least on the side of the British, no war was actually acknowledged. By the time the truce was declared in July 1921, approximately 2300 Auxiliaries, and around 10,000 Black and Tans, had been recruited for service in Ireland, in addition to the regular police and crown forces. The total number who served during the war was probably around 40,000. In addition, there were around 15,000 members of the IRA, although the number of those actively engaged in conflict was approximately 3000. Given that much of the military activity was confined to particular regions, the picture is one of intense activity, and troop saturation in certain towns and areas. Dublin, and south and central Munster (especially Cork, Kerry, Limerick and Tipperary) saw the greatest activity, although there were frequent engagements in the west and north midlands.

There has been some argument regarding what the IRA hoped to achieve through its guerrilla campaign. Some believed that a straightforward military victory was possible, and fought to that end. Others felt that the best that could be hoped for was a war of attrition which the British, already traumatised by the First World War, would eventually abandon. Others still believed that the British, with vast military resources and finance, could not be defeated as a fighting force, but might eventually tire of the great expenditure required to keep the situation under control, and negotiate a settlement. There is no doubt that financial considerations played a part in Lloyd George's eventual decision to call a truce: the war was expensive, and showed no signs of halting, despite his confident assertion in November 1920 that 'we have murder by the throat' in Ireland. But other pressures were being brought to bear on the Prime Minister and his cabinet. There was considerable Irish-American disquiet at the conduct of the war on the part of the British. On 3 June 1919, a report by the Irish-American 'Friends of

Irish Freedom' had been published and, even allowing for its partisan perspective, aroused condemnation of British tactics. This was followed by the American Commission on Conditions in Ireland of 1920–1921, which took statements from a broad range of witnesses, and caused further embarrassment for the British government. There was also a commission of enquiry by the Labour Party in autumn 1920 which undermined support in Britain itself. It was highly unlikely that the IRA would defeat the crown forces, but neither was it likely that the government would succeed in eliminating the IRA. As the war progressed, it became increasingly clear that this was no fleeting rebellion or Irish initiative which could be easily contained, as had happened in the past. Both sides were locked in conflict which did not suggest a rapid or easily achievable victory.

The British government nevertheless pressed ahead with a combination of military action and constitutional initiative. At the end of February, the Government of Ireland Bill was introduced in the House of Commons. This measure, a concrete form of the Home Rule Bill promised in 1914, allowed for the establishment of two governing bodies in Ireland, one north and one south. These Home Rule parliaments in Dublin and Belfast would liaise through an Irish Council, which, it was proposed, would deal with matters of common interest, and eventually settle the question of partition. This measure eventually became law as the Government of Ireland Act, passed in December 1920. Although its passage was largely ignored in the south of the country, for the practical reason that nationalists now accepted the Dáil as the real Parliament of Ireland, it was of much more immediate importance in Belfast, where unionists, for the most part reluctantly, accepted its provisions as the best means of avoiding a Home Rule Parliament for the whole of the country (see below, p. 69). In any case, the situation in the south appeared to be moving beyond control, a fact which diverted attention away from any constitutional settlement. In March, Tomás MacCurtain, the Lord Mayor of Cork and IRA commandant, was shot dead in his home, apparently by members of the RIC. His deputy, Terence MacSwiney, succeeded to both the Lord Mayorship and command of the 1st Cork IRA brigade. MacSwiney immediately became a focus of attention by the crown forces, and was arrested and detained in Brixton Prison. He began a hunger strike, which ended in his death after seventy-four days on 25 October, drawing further national as well as international criticism upon the British government. Ireland's situation was attracting increasing attention outside of the British Isles. Irish-Americans, in particular, maintained a steady pressure upon their government to urge Irish independence, but countries such as India also watched closely, and nationalists there hoped that a successful Irish campaign might provide a useful example for themselves. It was also in India that an extraordinary event took place, indicating how far concern for the situation at home had spread. In June, members of the Connaught Rangers, stationed at Jullundur in the Punjab, mutinied in protest at events in Ireland. Although the mutiny was swiftly repressed, with one man executed and many imprisoned, it was an indication of the potential for repercussion which Ireland held.

The IRA was less active in Ulster than in other parts of the country, but the north also saw considerable disturbances throughout 1920. Sectarian tensions, which had been evident before the First World War, revived in the most dramatic and horrific of ways. The first half of 1920 saw rioting and clashes with police, and resulted in the driving of Catholic families from Banbridge, Dromore and Belfast. Catholic workmen were expelled violently from shipyards in Belfast, and scores fled south. In response, the Dáil initiated the so-called Belfast Boycott in August, whereby goods manufactured, or even simply emanating from Belfast, were to be boycotted throughout the country. Trains driving south were subject to attack and their contents destroyed. The mood in the north, especially in Belfast, did not improve as the year advanced. In August, District Inspector O.R. Swanzy, whom the IRA believed to be closely involved in the death of Tomás MacCurtain, and who had been moved to Lisburn following the official enquiry, was murdered. His death was followed by attacks upon nationalists in the town, and disturbances spread to Belfast, leading to rioting and murder. The Ulster Unionist Council had accepted the Government of Ireland Bill in March, and in November began recruiting to the Special Constabulary Force. This was divided into three classes, a full-time, a part-time, and an emergency force (A, B and C), and the fact that many of those who enlisted were members of the Ulster Volunteers did little to allay Catholic and nationalist fears regarding the likely political coloration of the new force.

Back in the south, in August 1920, the Restoration of Order in Ireland Act became law. This was an attempt to bring the country under control, by allowing extraordinary powers to the crown forces to arrest and detain any individual suspected of illegal activity. It was now a crime to be associated with any banned organisation, which by this time covered most bodies even vaguely associated with political or cultural nationalism. It provided for imprisonment without trial, trial by court martial, and gave military tribunals precedence over civil. All this signalled that the military had been given carte blanche to restore order by whatever means they chose, and that the normal rights of citizens had been suspended. There was furthermore an increasing policy of unofficial reprisal by troops, who responded to assaults upon their forces with attacks upon known or suspected IRA men and their families. Although not actually condoned by the government, there was a decided lack of effort to limit reprisals, and many were convinced that it was being encouraged from the heart of government. Arrests became increasingly common, as did deaths in custody, and in suspicious circumstances. Civilians were caught up in direct conflict in increasing numbers, and atrocities became facts of everyday life. There were also concerted attacks by troops on cooperative creameries in rural areas, in an attempt to vividly demonstrate the economic consequences of war. Other startling demonstrations of force occurred in an attack by the Black and Tans on the towns of Balbriggan, Co. Dublin and Mallow, Co. Cork in September, and in the centre of Cork City in December 1920. There was massive destruction at both times – it is estimated that two and a half million pounds' worth of damage was caused in Cork, and the perpetrators were believed to be continuing in service unpunished. Other towns such as Galway, Tuam and Carrick-on-Shannon were also attacked, but with somewhat less devastating results. The accounts of attack and counter-attack from this period are graphic and distressing, but there were a number of particular incidents which stood alone in a depressing catalogue. The most dramatic occurred on 21 November, which became known as 'Bloody Sunday'. Michael Collins had become increasingly worried about the activities of a group of British intelligence agents in Dublin, and was determined to eliminate them. On the morning of 21 November, fourteen of these men were shot dead in their homes. Although Collins believed that their deaths were a necessary part of the war, it is likely that this action would have raised some criticism of Irish policy were it not for what happened that same afternoon, when the Black and Tans opened fire on the crowd at a Gaelic football match in Croke Park, Dublin, killing twelve people and injuring sixty. On the same day, two IRA men, Peadar Clancy and Dick McKee, died while in custody in Dublin Castle, allegedly while trying to escape. It would appear that from this point on, neither side was prepared to observe what might be described as the rules of war. The end of the month saw an attack on an auxiliary patrol in Kilmichael, Co. Cork, in which eighteen soldiers died. Although the Government of Ireland Act came into force on 23 December, it seemed already dead in the water as far as the south of Ireland was concerned. Settlement would apparently be won by force, or not at all.

The start of 1921, which also marked the third phase of the war, appeared remarkably inauspicious. On 1 January, seven houses in Co. Cork were destroyed as part of the British government's new policy of reprisal against IRA attacks. The war appeared to be continuing at the same furious pace, and with the same viciousness. On 28 February, for example, the execution of six republicans in Cork led to the assassination of six British soldiers in the city later that day. Although this sort of action implies stalemate, with atrocities merely matched by each side, in fact the situation looked set to grow a great deal worse. Under the terms of the Government of Ireland Act, elections were to be held in May to the northern and southern parliaments, the members taking their seats for the opening in June. If, however, less than half of the elected members were present, the Parliament would be dissolved and the relevant part of the country would be ruled as a crown colony. Given the Sinn Féin policy of abstention and the existence of the Dáil, it was more than likely that this is precisely what would happen, leaving the British government with the grim prospect of escalating the war dramatically, since a declaration that the south was now a crown colony would undoubtedly provoke a ferocious backlash against the British. It was for this reason, among many others – the protracted nature of the war, international opinion, high costs – that tentative contacts were made at the end of 1920 to explore the possibility of a truce. In these early days, the British government was adamant that a truce could only take place if the IRA surrendered, an impossible demand as far as the majority of nationalists were concerned. These efforts, conducted principally through members of the Catholic clergy, met with failure, but established a number of crucial links between the British government and Dáil members, in particular de Valera. Newly arrived from America, de Valera had the advantage of being largely unconnected with the actual execution of the military campaign of 1919–1920. Michael Collins on the other hand literally had a price on his head, a fact which made negotiation with the British difficult, to say the least. Attempts were again made in March and April 1921, and, in May, de Valera met with Sir James Craig to explore the possibility of links between the two parts of the island. Craig was elected leader of the Ulster Unionist Council upon Edward Carson's resignation in February, and was about to become Prime Minister of the Northern Irish Parliament. The two men found little common ground, dashing the very slim hope that the problem could be resolved within Ireland.

In line with the requirements of the Government of Ireland Act, candidates presented themselves for nomination to the two parliaments on 13 May. In a staggering, but not entirely surprising, development, all the candidates for the southern Parliament were returned unopposed, and comprised 124 standing for Sinn Féin, and four independents, who were in fact unionist candidates, standing for the University of Dublin. Through a decision which was to limit their political strength in subsequent years, labour had agreed not to nominate candidates in order to allow Sinn Féin a clean sweep. In the north, nominations and then elections (on 24 May) returned a predominantly unionist parliament, with forty gaining seats, along with twelve nationalists. Craig appointed his cabinet in early June, and the Northern Ireland Parliament was ready to function. In the meantime, the south had seen continued clashes with military forces, and a clear intent on the part of the newly elected Sinn Féin members to ignore the requirement to establish a southern Parliament. It looked as though the country was about to be plunged into further chaos when an unexpected opportunity for peace suddenly presented itself. King George V addressed the Northern Ireland Parliament at Belfast City Hall on 22 June, and made a moving speech in which he appealed for peace in the country. He asked that 'all Irishmen . . . stretch out the hand of forbearance and conciliation, to forgive and forget and to join in making for the land which they love a new era of peace, contentment and goodwill.' As a central figure, yet one without party ties, the King allowed for the articulation of a British desire to end the conflict, while avoiding a climb-down by government. Lloyd George contacted de Valera almost immediately to suggest a truce, an overture which made no mention of surrender. After some negotiation, the agreed truce began on 11 July 1921. The final phase of the Anglo-Irish War was over.

CHAPTER FIVE

The Treaty and its consequences, December 1921

The Treaty agreed between the British government and the representatives of Dáil Éireann in December 1921 marks a momentous development in modern Irish history. After the intense struggle, political and military, which had taken place in the previous three years, and the lengthy build-up to insurrection from the early years of the century, the claims of the Irish to independence were finally taken seriously. However, although the British government implicitly recognised both the Dáil and its claims by offering to negotiate a peace settlement, this did not mean that the Irish had won an unambiguous victory. There was the issue of the six north-eastern counties, which had governmental assurances over their continued existence within the United Kingdom. There was also the dangerously fragmented nature of Irish government. Although each individual was committed to breaking the link with Britain, they differed greatly in terms of the extent to which they were prepared to compromise. There were tensions between key figures which were accommodated easily enough in the context of Irish opposition to Britain, but were potentially far more disruptive once the country was faced with governing itself. Finally, when Lloyd George offered to negotiate with the Irish, the key word was 'negotiate'. He was not admitting defeat, or surrendering, yet the astonishment in Ireland that the government was willing to discuss terms created an understandable sense of victory, which made the idea of a compromise on the question of a Republic impossible.

Having said that, the invitation to discuss the situation did represent a remarkable victory for the Irish. With a tiny guerrilla army, poorly equipped, they had finally forced a world power to take their demands seriously. It is therefore worth considering the reasons for Britain's decision to negotiate with the Irish. One of the most important was the damage which the increasingly vicious campaign in Ireland was having on the British reputation abroad. In particular, opinion in America was turning decidedly against the policy of official as well as unofficial reprisals, even among those politicians who had no association with Ireland. Of course, the Irish-American community and their leaders had long been critical of British policy, a feeling strengthened by the frequent propaganda trips taken by Irish leaders throughout the United States. Women in particular were active in this area, and figures such as Hanna Sheehy Skeffington, Constance Markievicz, Muriel MacSwiney and many others undertook nationwide lecture tours, describing the impact of British policy on Irish civilians. American support was crucial for Britain in the post-war years, yet the Irish situation was in danger of alienating it. Within Britain itself, there was a desire to resolve the apparently intractable Irish problem, and to enter properly a period of peace. The war-weariness in the country demanded some manner of settlement, for although the Irish conflict did not disrupt life in the manner of the Great War, it still represented a drain on resources, and continued a sense of conflict which many felt should have ended in 1918. Moreover, as the Irish kept reminding the British, Britain had gone to war 'in defence of small nations', yet she persisted in maintaining heavy-handed control over a nation which demanded its independence. The Labour Party Commission of Enquiry, which gathered information about atrocities in Ireland in the autumn of 1920, further fuelled criticism of government policy at home. Finally there was a desire in certain quarters to simply abandon Ireland to its fate. Its possession was too expensive, and too troublesome, to make it worth keeping. All this might suggest that Lloyd George was in some way forced into the decision to offer a truce. This is far from the case. Despite the factors listed above, Britain was obviously the far more powerful country, capable of prosecuting the war to an extent which would make an Irish defeat inevitable. Whatever optimistic nationalists might think, Lloyd George still held the stronger hand, and overtures to the Irish meant that he was merely willing to explore possibilities, not give in to demands. Nevertheless, he had moved considerably from his earlier position as far as a truce was concerned. Most importantly from the Dáil's perspective, he dropped the precondition of surrender of arms, and placed no restrictions upon whom should represent the southerners. The offer of a truce was then followed by a lengthy and tortuous process of negotiation, in which de Valera attempted to assert his authority as President of Dáil Éireann by emphasising his own preconditions (that Craig should not be present at his talks with the British Prime Minister, and that a truce should be in place before he travelled to London, not starting when he arrived there). The exclusion of Craig was actually an irrelevance – he had already secured an agreement with Lloyd George, unbeknownst to de Valera, that the six northern counties would never be coerced into any Home Rule Parliament with Dublin. Finally, at noon on 11 July 1921, the truce came into operation, and the Anglo-Irish War was over.

From the Irish perspective, the announcement that there were to be peace talks was greeted rapturously. There was widespread relief that the terrifying campaign would end, and a sense throughout the country that a significant victory had been won against great odds. The nation was optimistic about the outcome of any talks, and many argued that the Irish Republic, so long awaited, was about to be achieved. Many of the revolutionary leaders were also swept up in the popular mood, with Tom Barry believing that victory had already been won in 1921, and the negotiations were merely a means of confirming the Republic. Others, such as Liam Deasy, were stunned, amazed that the battle had come to such an abrupt and unexpected halt. The realists were cautious of proclaiming any victory however. Michael Collins, for example, realised that the most difficult part of the process was just beginning. He was, moreover, astonished that the British government had chosen this moment to begin negotiations. He was more aware than most of the pressure the IRA was under in terms of weaponry and personnel. He was eventually to tell the Chief Secretary that when the truce was called, he estimated that the Irish forces could not have lasted for more than three further weeks, so depleted were their resources. Others within the movement were also aware both of the state of the IRA and the fact that discussion implied compromise. They therefore regarded the truce not as a step towards a negotiated settlement, but as a breathing space within which the army would re-equip for a further struggle, which would win the Republic outright. It is at this point that the differing personalities of Collins and de Valera become more significant. Both were astute men, and both, in different ways, ruthless and charismatic leaders. However, where Collins was inclined to be almost brutally straightforward in his approach to politics, de Valera was notoriously circuitous, often masking his ultimate ambition behind a convoluted discourse and procedure. They were also, as the truce was called, the two most dominant figures on a stage peopled with activists of an exceptional calibre. De Valera had the prestige of 1916, and a growing reputation as a political figure. Collins had acquired an almost mythic status through his campaign during the Anglo-Irish War, and inspired a devoted following. What both men knew was that there would have to be compromise on the ideal of the Republic. The question was: Which of them would willingly be associated with that compromise?

This question came swiftly to the fore. For this first encounter, de Valera, along with Arthur Griffith, Robert Barton, Austin Stack and Erskine Childers, travelled to London. Michael Collins, despite his protests, was left at home, a decision made by de Valera, and one which provided an ominous pointer towards their future relationship. The visitors' high hopes were swiftly dashed by Lloyd George's limited offer. What he proposed for Ireland was Dominion status – limited independence in certain domestic matters, but with British control retained in crucial areas. For example, Britain would hold certain ports in Ireland which were regarded as central to her security. This was anathema to the Irish, as it meant the continued presence of British forces in Ireland. Ireland would also be responsible for a certain proportion of the British war debt, again an unsavoury proposal, implying as it did that the war had been a joint venture. Most importantly, any deal would have to recognise the validity of the northern Parliament, with no framework for its integration into any future Irish Parliament without its consent. This meant the acceptance of partition, as even the most optimistic republican realised that Craig's Parliament was most unlikely to voluntarily join the southern body. De Valera's instinct was to instantly reject this offer, but Lloyd George persuaded him to take it back to Dublin for discussion, adding that the only alternative was the resumption of war.

Predictably, the Dáil, meeting in full strength for the first time, decided to reject the offer. As a result of the truce, many members were newly released from prison, and not in the most amenable frame of mind for compromise. At its first meeting in August, de Valera's title was changed to 'President of the Irish Republic', a defiant gesture of faith in what form an Irish Parliament would take. All Dáil members now took an oath of allegiance to 'the Irish Republic and the Government of the Irish Republic', thereby tying themselves into a constitutional position with little room for manoeuvre. A new cabinet was formed, consisting of de Valera, Collins, Griffith, Brugha, Barton, Stack and Cosgrave. The political situation they faced was serious, but despite the uncompromising rhetoric there was apparently a willingness to bend a little on both sides. War did not in fact resume following the Dáil's rejection, but rather an intense period of discussion between de Valera and Lloyd George. Over the next two months, the two men discussed the apparently impossible task of reconciling two entirely contrary political positions, and it gradually emerged that de Valera reluctantly considered the possibility that an Irish Republic might not be immediately attainable. He therefore wanted to create a situation in which Ireland would be 'associated' with Britain, but not governed by her, a partial rather than a total break of the union. At home, he appeared to be preparing his colleagues, and the country at large, for compromise by stressing that they should not be tied irrevocably to the ideal of the Republic. Lloyd George, watching these developments closely, therefore invited de Valera to talks in London to formulate a peace settlement. The Irish President was now faced with the task of choosing his team.

To the astonishment of many of his contemporaries, and to the puzzlement of subsequent commentators, de Valera excluded himself from the delegation. He declared that as President he should not be engaged in negotiations, an argument that fell flat in the face of Lloyd George's key presence at the talks. It has been suggested that de Valera considered it better to remain at home in order to restrain the more uncompromising members of the cabinet such as Brugha, although again this is open to debate, since his presidential authority should in any case have been respected. One advantage of his remaining in Ireland was that the delegates would have to refer any proposals back to him, thereby giving them a breathing space from what would inevitably be a pressurised situation. However, even this strategy was hampered from the start. The delegates were formally charged by the Dáil with the power to 'negotiate and *conclude*' (my emphasis) a Treaty with the British government. However, before they left for London, they were instructed to refer any proposal back to Dublin for approval before signing. This mixed message was to have dire consequences. The final possible explanation for de Valera's absence is the harshest: he was fully aware that in agreeing to negotiate with the British, the ideal of the Republic was for the present unattainable. Despite British willingness to talk, it was inconceivable that they would agree to a fully fledged Republic: such a development would damage Britain's international reputation, be impossible to sell to unionist members at Westminster, and, most importantly, set a dangerous precedent for her other colonial possessions, in particular India. De Valera did not want to be the one who failed to deliver the Republic and to be put in the position of attempting to impose what many would regard as an unacceptable compromise on Ireland. Hard-liners in the Dáil would make the presentation of any deviation from the ideal extremely difficult.

The team which finally left for London, despite de Valera's absence, was one of talent. Arthur Griffith was at the head, supported by Michael Collins, Robert Barton, Gavan Duffy and Eamon Duggan. Although none were under any illusions about the scale of the task which lay before them, perhaps the most reluctant member was Collins. He had been persuaded to act against his better judgement, and it was only the fear that the entire process might be jeopardised, or unbalanced by republican hard-liners, that prompted him to go. No less than de Valera, or indeed the majority of the delegation and their entourage, he knew that the attainment of a republic was a slim possibility. The Irish were moreover facing the strongest possible team of British negotiators. In addition to the Prime Minster Lloyd George, there was Winston Churchill, Lord Birkenhead and Austen Chamberlain, all men with years of political experience behind them. It was a formidable challenge indeed.

Nevertheless, the British were also facing a difficult task. Lloyd George's government was a coalition, and he faced individuals within and outside his cabinet who regarded these peace talks with a great deal of suspicion. Unionist members were uniformly opposed to granting any form of independence, preferring to resume hostilities in Ireland rather than be seen to negotiate with those whom they regarded as terrorists. Indeed, as the talks were underway Lloyd George had to face a vote of censure within the House of Commons from unionist members: he and his cabinet survived, but it was a salutary reminder of the difficulty he faced in attempting to solve the Irish question. Although the Ulster unionists were relatively satisfied with their own Parliament, Craig had made it clear that any attempt to coerce them into an accommodation with the south would result in civil war. They had considerable support in Britain, and were capable of generating significant opposition to government.

The talks opened on 11 October 1921, and carried on, with breaks for the Irish to update Dáil colleagues, until 6 December. Both sides entered into discussion determined to hold to certain, apparently irreconcilable, principles. For the Irish, it was essential that if the talks broke down, they should break on the question of Ulster's future. The establishment of the northern Parliament represented the partition of the country, and the denial of the Republic. For the British, the key issue was Ireland's relationship to the crown. Ever fearful of the security implications which a hostile Ireland represented (especially one willing to create alliances with Britain's enemies, as had been threatened during the First World War), the British team was determined that any settlement was predicated upon an acceptance of British security interests, even if these interests directly impinged upon Irish internal affairs. In the event, this concern was expressed through two crucial elements in the negotiations. It was agreed that the British would retain certain Irish ports, namely Berehaven (Cork), Lough Swilly (Donegal), and Queenstown (Cork), in addition to facilities in Belfast Lough in order to protect her own security interests. Although this meant a continued British military presence in Ireland, the Irish accepted the condition relatively easily. Far more difficult was the question of the crown. The Irish were willing to belong to the Commonwealth, but not to allow any crown interference with the government of the country. The British wanted to know what precisely would be the relationship, and more importantly the obligations, of Irish citizens to the Empire. In the end, it was agreed that a system of reciprocal citizenship should exist, with the citizens of each country holding equal rights within each others' countries. This actually worked quite well in practice, as the years ahead were to prove, but at the time it still left the exact relationship of Ireland to the Empire undetermined.

As the talks advanced, it became clear that there were two principal sticking points, and that little movement seemed possible on either. One was the question of Ulster, the other the exact constitutional position of Ireland. Lloyd George entered into a series of discussions with Griffith over possible compromises, offering to attempt to persuade (with the implied threat of coercion) the Ulster unionists to come to an accommodation with the south in return for Irish movement on the question of the crown. Griffith, after some consultation with the delegation, agreed to recommend that Ireland should recognise the crown as head of the Association of Free States, and that she should join in 'free partnership' with the British Commonwealth. In an apparently innocuous amendment, which was in fact to have a far-reaching effect, the British team convinced Griffith to state that the 'free partnership' would be *within* the Commonwealth, thereby drawing Ireland into a far closer constitutional relationship than Griffith had envisaged. Attention now turned to what Lloyd George was prepared to offer on Ulster. Despite his suggestion that he would either force Craig to accept an accommodation with the south, or resign in protest, he did neither. Instead he presented the Irish delegates with a new proposal: a Boundary Commission would be established which would redraw the existing boundary between north and south. The Prime Minster argued persuasively that if the wishes of the people directly affected were considered, the portion left in the north would be too small to survive without union with the south, and that partition would therefore end through economic as well as political pressure. What he neglected to mention was that he had already privately assured Craig that the six counties would never be coerced by Westminster, and that whatever support was necessary to maintain its position within the United Kingdom would be forthcoming. Lloyd George extracted a promise in writing from Griffith that he would agree to the following: if the six counties refused to join an all-Ireland Parliament within a year, then the territory would be subject to the Boundary Commission. Griffith, believing that he was merely offering support to the Prime Minister in the face of unionist opposition in Parliament, and that the Boundary Commission remained a solely British initiative, agreed. This promise was to rebound on the Irish with devastating effect.

From mid-November to early December, although remarkable progress had been made, there still remained the unresolved question of Ireland's relationship to the crown. The Irish insisted that it should have no practical relevance within the country, and the British insisted that Ireland's citizens should, through the Dáil, take some form of an oath of allegiance which would protect British interests, and remove the implication that the British no longer had any presence in the country. The principal problem was Ireland's geographical proximity to Britain. Unlike Canada or Australia, it would be very easy for Britain to make her considerable presence felt in Ireland, and an oath of allegiance to the crown would have a far more binding and immediate effect. However, there was little time to consider the niceties of the question. At the start of negotiations, Lloyd George had promised Craig that negotiations would be finished, and a Treaty agreed (or rejected) by 6 December. This date had therefore been set as the end of discussions, and although in the cold light of day there appeared no reason why the deadline could not be extended, all had been working towards it. The Irish team returned to Dublin to take the final British offer to the cabinet. A lengthy debate ensued, with the delegates arguing that this settlement represented the best that could be achieved under the circumstances, and also claiming that, as was true, it represented a far more liberal arrangement than had ever been on offer before. Despite their own reluctance to accept any mention of the crown, most of the delegates agreed that it was impossible for the British to abandon this point entirely, and an Irish rejection would destroy the Boundary Commission, Ireland's only hope of altering the situation on partition. On the other hand, it was argued that this should be regarded as a mere opening manoeuvre, and that the British were bluffing when they said that the only alternative was war. What was unmistakable was that a republic was not even vaguely within grasp. After deep, and frequently highly personalised discussions, the Irish delegates were dispatched back to London, bearing a re-draft of the Oath of Allegiance by de Valera which emphasised the concept of external association rather than links within the Empire. On 4 December they again met with Lloyd George, whose own position appeared to have hardened in their absence.

The negotiations entered their final phase. The Irish were suffering from the effects both of exhaustion and the difficulty of maintaining unity in the face of intense disappointment over the emerging settlement. A point worth remembering is that none of the Irish team were satisfied with what had been achieved, and were in the difficult position of having to sell an agreement they themselves detested to a country which had far higher expectations. The group was riven with internal disagreements, with individuals such as Childers proving dangerously inflexible over the loss of the Republic. The only point upon which the Irish team felt it could exert pressure was Ulster, and the necessity for Craig to agree to the crucial point of Irish unity, if the Irish would accept the Oath of Allegiance. Even this was undermined by Lloyd George's timely brandishing of Griffith's agreement to the Boundary Commission, leaving the delegates with little scope for movement.

The final crucial point now remained. The Irish produced de Valera's revised Oath of Allegiance, which the British rejected as too explicit a statement of external allegiance to be acceptable. The British negotiators did however agree to amend their own suggested oath, which now read:

> I . . . do solemnly swear true faith and allegiance to the constitution of the Irish Free State as by law established, and that I will be faithful to H. M. King George V, his heirs and successors by law, in virtue of the common citizenship of Ireland with Great Britain and her adherence to and membership of the group of nations forming the British Commonwealth of Nations.

This oath, and the remainder of the agreement which established British and Irish responsibilities with regard to economics, politics and law, offered Dominion status to Ireland, a far cry from what many had hoped for. Lloyd George then delivered a psychologically damaging blow. Theatrically presenting two sealed letters, he asked which of them – one confirming that the Treaty had been signed, the other telling of Irish rejection of the deal – he should send to James Craig. The Irish retired to consider their decision, and, after almost eight hours of the most traumatic debate, agreed to sign the Articles of Agreement for a Treaty between Britain and Ireland. This momentous event begs an obvious question: Why did the delegates sign the Treaty without referring it back to the Dáil for discussion? It is not an easy question to answer. It may be partly explained at least by the tremendous pressure the Irish delegates found themselves under. Lloyd George's melodramatic ultimatum was well timed, and the relative inexperience of the Irish negotiators may be seen in their general acceptance of it. More important however is the fact that Collins and Griffith at least believed that they had extracted the maximum possible concession out of the British, and that even if Lloyd George's words were mere bluff, there was little more that the Irish might expect to achieve. Finally, the delegates believed themselves to be empowered to sign on behalf of the Dáil, because of the ambiguous instructions given to them in October. Whatever the reason, the Treaty was signed at 2.30 a.m. Collins' assessment of the event is often quoted, but is worth repeating here, both as an indication of how uncertain the delegates themselves were about what they had achieved, and for its unfortunately prophetic statement:

> Think – what have I got for Ireland? Something which she has wanted for the past 700 years. Will anyone be satisfied at the bargain? Will anyone? I tell you this – early this morning I signed my death warrant. I thought at the time how odd, how ridiculous – a bullet may just as well have done the job five years ago.

So what in fact had been achieved? Looked at rationally, and from a great historical distance, it is clear that both sides had moved substantially from their earlier positions. In this sense the Treaty was a true compromise, although the sense of disappointment, especially for the Irish, masked this considerable achievement. The Treaty went far beyond Home Rule in terms of the freedoms offered to Ireland. Although Canada was the model frequently referred to during the negotiations, and indeed cited as the official comparison in the Treaty itself, the Irish position was quite different. Most importantly, Ireland would assume control over her own finances, have a distinct and independent defence force, and the right to regulate her own trade, even with Britain. She would have her own Parliament, and the official British presence would be reduced to a Governor-General. On the other hand, British military forces would remain in Ireland at the so-called Treaty ports, Ireland would have to pay a share of the British war debt, and partition was made practically a certainty. From the British perspective, the Treaty represented significant concessions to Ireland, but, on balance, protected her interests relatively well. It was important to ensure continued conservative and unionist support at home, which had been achieved through the safeguards offered to the new northern state, and security concerns had been addressed through the retention of the ports. The settlement would restore British prestige abroad without involving her in significant expenditure or domestic political controversy. Those political leaders blessed with a degree of foresight expressed concern over the long-term implications of partition, but they were easily dismissed in the generally positive atmosphere. It now remained to be seen how the agreement would be received by the public of both countries.

The Treaty had a mixed reception in Ireland. For many, it represented a huge advance in Anglo-Irish relations, and was considered a remarkable achievement with so few resources. For others, it was a bitter disappointment, bringing not merely partition, but the loss of the Republic. However, the specifics were not known by the country at large for some time. It was the reaction of the cabinet, which met on 8 December, which provided an ominous inkling of the trouble to come. In a heated session, the delegates explained why they had come to sign the Treaty, and presented their arguments as to its worth. This was of little avail as far as individuals such as Brugha were concerned, and when the cabinet voted on the issue, it divided in a predictable manner. Collins, Griffith, Barton and Cosgrave voted to accept; Brugha, de Valera and Stack voted against. Despite their nominal unity as cabinet members, it was instantly clear that Collins and de Valera would lead the two opposing factions within the Dáil, once the Treaty was presented there for debate.

A tortuous and bitter debate opened on 14 December and lasted for almost a month, with a break for Christmas. The recorded debates reveal the great depth of feeling on the topic, and although at times rational argument may have been obscured by emotion, they indicate how personally important was the question. One could argue that these few weeks determined the whole future of the country: they certainly set the political climate for the remainder of the century. The debates were at times confused, ranging over a series of issues, but they can be reduced to a small number of key questions. Did the Treaty really represent the best deal which could be achieved at this time, and what kind of relationship would pertain between Britain and Ireland, if the Treaty were approved by the Dáil? The key point to remember is that not one individual in the Dáil believed that Irish ambitions had been fully achieved by the Treaty. Rather, it was a question of whether, given the circumstances under which the Anglo-Irish War had been fought, and the relatively weak position to which Irish forces were now reduced, the Treaty was worth accepting. For Griffith, Collins and their supporters, the position was simple: the Treaty was far from ideal, but it represented both a huge achievement for Ireland, and provided the basis upon which further freedoms could be won. As Collins was to famously note in his address to the Assembly, the Treaty gave 'not the ultimate freedom that all nations aspire and develop to, but the freedom to achieve it'. Both men argued that they had not in fact gone to London in the belief that a republic was on offer, but in order to negotiate a settlement, a position which automatically implied that their ultimate objective could not be achieved.

Throughout the debates, de Valera consistently rejected the London delegates' arguments, stating that they had failed to secure what they had been instructed to. However, when the cabinet met in private session on 15 and 16 December, de Valera produced a document, in effect a minor rewrite of the Treaty, which he deemed to be more acceptable. Known as 'Document No. 2', it offered Britain the same defence conditions as the Treaty, but limited them for five years. With regard to partition, he came up with a solution which was classically de Valerian. It accepted partition in order to prevent civil war, but refused to recognise that any part of the country could be alienated from the Irish state. Thus the country would be theoretically united, while partitioned in fact. Griffith's and Collins' response was dismissive, but they argued that the document should be made public in order that the Dáil, and the country at large, be shown that what de Valera himself proposed was a compromise of the republican ideal. De Valera refused, stating that as the document had been presented in confidence it could not to be made available to the public. The debates continued. Some of the most passionate and personalised speeches were given by women members in opposition to the Treaty. Constance Markievicz, Mary MacSwiney, Margaret Pearse (mother of Patrick) and Kathleen Clarke (widow of Tom) all spoke at length against the Articles of Agreement. They have been critically assessed by many historians, and indeed by their contemporaries, for the wildness of their speeches (and in the case of MacSwiney, its duration). However, their actions should be put in the context of the roles played by women during the Anglo-Irish War, and the fact that, because women had been exceptionally active and involved, they felt they had even more of a stake in the outcome. There was also a certain hostility towards the women which may stem from a belief that they were flouting traditional roles. This was accepted at a time when the country was relatively united in a common cause, but provided an easy target when crisis loomed. Their language, although intemperate, was not particularly different from that of many of their male colleagues, and reflected the beliefs of many other republican women – Cumann na mBan was to overwhelmingly reject the Treaty.

The most decisive period for the future of the Treaty came not when the Dáil was in session, but during the Christmas adjournment. When the members returned to their constituencies, they found that the public was surprisingly positive about the settlement, as were the churches, business interests and most public bodies. When the Dáil met again on 3 January, many who had been genuinely undecided returned largely in favour, and Collins took advantage of this slightly altered mood to insist on drawing the debates to a close. Recognising that some positions were irreconcilable, he suggested that those opposed to the Treaty simply abstain from voting, to allow the provisional government to assume control from the British, and then work out a reasonable solution. This proposal, extraordinary as it seems in terms of general political life, actually reflects the fact that most Dáil members were genuinely concerned for the country's future rather than personal political gain, and also emphasises the close relationship which existed between those individuals who had so recently been on the same side in the Anglo-Irish War. De Valera was instantly opposed, realising how difficult it would be to reform or even reject an Irish Parliament once it had been established. However, recognising the turn which the situation had taken, he attempted to convince the population of the feasibility of rejecting the Treaty by returning to Document No. 2, or at least a modified version of it. In it he proposed that the Oath of Allegiance to the King be dropped in favour of the phrase: 'That, for the purposes of the Association, Ireland shall recognise His Britannic Majesty as head of the Association', the Association placing Ireland outside the Commonwealth, and therefore beyond any suggestion of crown control. Had the Dáil accepted this alternative, which they were not in fact officially discussing, it would certainly have been rejected by the British. However, members were in fact moving steadily towards the vote on the Treaty, and on 7 January, it finally came. The House was almost evenly divided, with sixty-four votes in favour and fifty-seven against. Despite the fact that the decision had finally been made, the scene was one of upset and confusion. De Valera resigned as President of the Republic, and the election for the presidency of the Dáil took place, with Griffith defeating de Valera by two votes. In the atmosphere of heightened emotion, Griffith declared his respect and affection for de Valera, who responded by saying that he would support the provisional government, but, ominously, without compromising his ideals. This magnanimity was soon to be sorely tested.

If the Treaty were to be accepted in the country as a whole, the response of other interest groups was crucial. Perhaps the most important of these was the IRA. Although generally committed to the republican ideal, IRA leaders also knew how poorly equipped the army was to resume hostilities. Initially, and largely owing to Collins' personal popularity, the GHQ of the IRA agreed in a meeting to support the decision of the Dáil, which looked likely to ratify the Agreement. Equally importantly, Collins used his influence within the IRB to urge acceptance of the Treaty, and on 12 December the Supreme Council of the organisation issued a statement to IRB divisional leaders which supported the Treaty. IRB members in the Dáil were to be allowed a free vote, but the statement put them in a difficult position. Although IRB influence within the Dáil was limited, and was probably far less pervasive than contemporaries believed, de Valera was furious that this secret organisation had any role to play in the crucial question. These manoeuvres did not mean however that Collins could confidently rely upon the support of the army. Despite the assurances of the Minister of Defence, Richard Mulcahy, that the army would be loyal to the new state, there were ominous signs of fracture. Individuals such as Liam Lynch and Ernie O'Malley, both of whom commanded intense loyalty from their men, declared their opposition to the Treaty, and it was feared that their stance would provoke a split in the ranks. All were aware of the militant precedent which had been set in recent Irish politics, and of the narrow margin by which the Treaty had been passed in the Dáil. It was this history, and the fact that a generation had come to maturity in a context of political advance through violence, that presented a worrying precedent for the new Ireland.

CHAPTER SIX

The Civil War, January 1922 to May 1923

In January 1922, it was possible to point to the remarkable achievements of the past few years. Despite enormous odds, a treaty had been negotiated with the British government which re-established an Irish Parliament, saw the creation of an Irish army, and the withdrawal of crown forces from most of the country. However, even the most optimistic of commentators could not escape the signs of disappointment and discontent which emerged immediately after the last session of the Dáil. Although all members had vowed to support their country, interpretations of what that country might be were vastly different. This was immediately clear when on 14 January the Southern Ireland Parliament (in fact, precisely the same as the Dáil, with the addition of the four members for Dublin University, as demanded by the Government of Ireland Act of 1920) met for the first time. It was headed by a new ministry, led by Arthur Griffith as President and including Michael Collins, Richard Mulcahy, George Gavan Duffy, William Cosgrave, Kevin O'Higgins, Ernest Blythe, Eamon Duggan, P.J. Hogan, Joseph McGrath and Michael Hayes. De Valera and the other anti-Treaty members did not attend, and although the Treaty was formally approved, it was clear that a significant minority opposed it. This meeting also established a provisional government, of which Collins was Chairman, and whose members were Cosgrave, O'Higgins, McGrath, Duggan and Hogan (all members of the Dáil Ministry) as well as Eoin Mac-Neill and Finian Lynch. The overlap was inevitable under the circumstances, and reflected the desire on both Collins' and Griffith's part to hold pro- and anti-Treaty forces together as far as possible.

This desire to avoid open conflict was expressed in every aspect of the interim government. Collins in particular was under dreadful pressure to ensure that there was no irreparable breach between the two sides, but he had the added difficulty of being under close observation from Westminster. The terms of the Government of Ireland Act required that the Treaty be approved by the Dáil, which it had by a slim majority, but also that it be put to the people in the form of a general election to the new Parliament, which would replace the provisional government. The election would reflect public opinion on the Treaty, and on the future form of government, as it was also intended that a draft constitution for the Free State, as the 26-county unit was to be known, would be circulated in time for the election. Collins and his colleagues had therefore to devise practical formulas which would reassure the British that the terms of the Treaty were being fulfilled, ease republican fears regarding the extent to which their ideals had been compromised, and present the country with a form of government that reflected what they presumed had been offered by the Treaty. Any one of these groups was capable of destroying the fragile accord in the country, although the republicans, now also known as the 'irregulars', represented by far the greatest threat. As the weeks passed, the provisional government had yet another problem to add to their list: Northern Ireland.

The government of Northern Ireland which had been established under the Government of Ireland Act of 1920 had been functioning reasonably well. However, the attacks upon Catholics which had led to murder and hundreds fleeing their homes looked set to begin again. Although the truce had led to relative peace in the south, it actually marked the start of the worst period of violence in the north, peaking in May 1922 when eighty individuals were murdered. Between mid-1920 and the summer of 1922, approximately 550 people had been killed, 300 of whom were Catholic, 170 Protestant, and around eighty members of the crown forces. Belfast, a city with a long-standing reputation for sectarianism, was the centre of the conflict, with the majority of deaths occurring there. Collins believed that northern Catholic nationalists would be eventually protected by the outcome of the Boundary Commission, which would transfer regions and counties with those majorities into the Free State, but in the interim he attempted to calm the situation by striking an agreement with Craig when they met on 21 January. In return for ending the boycott of goods from Belfast, Craig agreed to protect Catholics from attack. However, assaults and intimidation continued, and the IRA began a new campaign against the northern state. Initially, its focus was on business interests, but its actions began a vicious cycle of reprisal and counter-reprisal which threatened to destabilise the country. Craig's forces were more than willing to implement equally vicious responses to attack, and they had the advantage of official sanction. Ironically, some historians have seen in the IRA campaign an opportunity for the pro- and anti-Treaty camps to unite against a clearly identifiable enemy, thereby easing the situation in the south, but the preoccupation with the threatened civil war ruled out collective action for the immediate future. Collins in particular was distressed by the appalling events in Northern Ireland, and protested to Craig, to no avail. Craig's response, goaded by the hardliners in his cabinet, was to introduce the Civil Authorities (Special Powers) Bill in early April 1922, giving unprecedented powers to the Northern Ireland government, more generous, indeed, than the measures originally introduced by Lloyd George under the Restoration of Order in Ireland Act, itself regarded as an extraordinary measure. Under the Act, suspects could be detained indefinitely without trial, special courts could impose sentences of imprisonment or even death, and curfews were imposed. Although the Bill was originally intended to be effective for only one year, it was renewed annually and then made permanent in 1933, allowing the Northern Ireland state to be governed under emergency, and draconian, powers. That such an exceptional measure was deemed necessary to govern the state illustrates the tensions inherent in a unionist-ruled region with a significant nationalist minority, and provides a pointer towards the outbreak of the 'Troubles' in Northern Ireland in the 1960s. On 5 April, just two days before the Civil Authorities Bill was passed, the Royal Ulster Constabulary had been formed, and this force, in addition to the Special Constabulary already established, meant that Northern Ireland appeared to be turning into a police state. By June there were 50,000 regular and part-time policemen, the great majority of whom were Protestant. Sir Henry Wilson, recently appointed as Northern Ireland's military adviser, fulfilled his reputation as a militant unionist, leading many Catholic nationalists in the state to despair for their futures there.

In the south, even the most obvious causes for celebration were marred by internal conflict. Once the Dáil had ratified the Treaty, the British government began withdrawing its forces from barracks and depots around the country. Collins had formally assumed responsibility for the country's administrative centre when Dublin Castle was handed over on 15 January. The Civil Service take-over was a great deal easier than had been anticipated, with the vast majority of employees remaining in post under the new admin-istration (300 members voluntarily transferred to Belfast, and 21,000 continued at work). The withdrawal of military personnel, although the most obvious signal of a transfer of power, caused the greatest problems. As the British soldiers and auxiliary forces left, there were frequent struggles between pro- and anti-Treaty units, espe-cially in rural areas, as each sought to occupy fortified buildings and secure arms. This was a reflection of worrying developments in February and March. On 5 February, a Cumann na mBan con-vention had been called to discuss the Treaty. Although the execu-tive had already signalled their rejection (by twenty-four votes to two), the membership was to have an open vote. At the meeting Mary MacSwiney proposed a resolution which asked members to reaffirm their allegiance to the Republic, and reimpose the Belfast boycott: 419 members voted in favour, with sixty-three against. The clear stance taken by Cumann na mBan was a worry for the provisional government – it was all too aware of the significant role played by the women in the Anglo-Irish War, and of the danger in that expertise and support now being turned against them. On 26 March the IRA met, despite an attempted ban by Richard Mulcahy. Many pro-Treaty members were absent, out of loyalty to Mulcahy, and the meeting was dominated by staunch anti-Treaty men such as Rory O'Connor, Liam Lynch, Liam Mellows and Ernie O'Malley. The outcome was somewhat predictable – the provisional government was rejected, a new oath to the Republic was taken which severed the association between the Republic and the new Dáil, and an army executive was established from which, and solely which, the IRA would now take orders. Just as Mulcahy had feared, the convention had effectively established a militant opposition. Almost immediately the IRA took action. In addition to conducting raids for arms throughout the country, units also launched attacks upon banks and post offices, seizing funds in the name of the Republic. The most important development came on 14 April, when an IRA unit led by Rory O'Connor occupied the Four Courts in the centre of Dublin, and declared it to be the head-quarters of the executive of the anti-Treaty IRA forces. This was a blatant challenge to the authority of the provisional government, and one which would be difficult to ignore. Collins and Griffith were placed in an impossible position. Anxious at all costs to avoid driving the country to civil war, they feared that an attack on the Four Courts would galvanise even those anti-Treaty elements who were for the moment prepared to stay their hands. Collins in particular was reluctant to move against his former comrades in arms, because he feared provoking a violent reaction of which he, far more than Griffith, understood the consequences. However, to simply ignore the occupation was to imply approval of their actions, and also suggest weakness on the provisional government's part. It was not a dilemma which was to be easily resolved. Against this backdrop, the provisional government began recruiting for a new police force to replace the Royal Irish Constabulary. To their credit, and to the surprise of some contemporaries, the government made the decision to create an unarmed force, a policy which has remained to the present day. The organisation was known as the Garda Síochána (Civic Guard), and was drawn from the general population as well as men who had been active in the Anglo-Irish War.

In the meantime, yet another potentially destabilising force emerged. Eamon de Valera, having retreated to lick his wounds after the dissolution of the Dáil, announced the establishment on 16 March of a new political party with himself at the head: Cumann na Poblachta (League of the Republic). This party largely consisted of anti-Treaty Dáil members, and although it was ostensibly constitutional and democratic, de Valera appeared to signal otherwise in a series of inflammatory speeches. He famously declared that it might be necessary to 'wade through Irish blood, through the blood of the soldiers of the Irish Government and through, perhaps, the blood of some of the members of the Government' in order to achieve 'Irish freedom'. Statements such as these convinced many members of the provisional government – and have convinced many historians since – that de Valera contributed significantly to the rush towards civil war. There is no doubt that his words carried great weight – he was after all one of the heroes of the 1916 Rising. However, it is also possible to read these speeches as evidence of political desperation on de Valera's part. The anti-Treaty initiative had been seized by O'Connor and Lynch, and de Valera may have wished to appear equally resolute, a stance which would require strong words, even if the speaker did not favour especially strong actions. It is however easy to overestimate de Valera's authority during this period. Because of his lifelong dominance in Irish politics after 1928, some commentators have presumed he was a key player during the civil war. What is in fact clear is that the anti-Treaty army members operated in almost complete independence (and with almost complete disregard) of de Valera. Once the war began he was swiftly sidelined, and his attempts to halt the war were largely ignored. It was only when the principal army leaders such as Cathal Brugha, Rory O'Connor and Liam Lynch were killed that de Valera re-emerged as a figure to whom the irregulars listened. The population at large continued to hold him in high esteem throughout the period, but they were not the ones prosecuting the war.

By the early summer of 1922 there were five significant political forces in Ireland. Three were legally established, and pro-Treaty to greater or lesser degrees: the provisional government, the Dáil, and the government of Northern Ireland. Two were anti-Treaty, and rather less predictable: Cumann na Poblachta and the IRA executive. All awaited the outcome of the general election, which would explicitly express the wishes of the people as far as the Treaty was concerned. Driven by his overwhelming desire to maintain unity, however tenuous, Collins set to work on ensuring as far as possible that the election would not provoke either of the anti-Treaty camps into action. In May the 'Army Document', as it came to be known, was issued jointly by pro- and anti-Treaty forces. This was an initiative from the military in both camps, and is an indication of how desperate even the now-divided army was to prevent civil war. It called for unity, and proposed that the election should be agreed; that is, that both sides should be allowed to secure representation in whatever government would emerge after the elections. This, it was hoped, would ensure that no single body would unilaterally seize power, or seek to disrupt government. But Collins was to go even further. Recognising that de Valera would inevitably emerge as a key political figure, he met with the Cumann na Poblachta leader on 20 May, and the two men agreed the so-called 'election pact'. The terms of the agreement were relatively simple. The new Dáil would consist of pro- and anti-Treaty members in approximately the same numbers as existed in the present Dáil. This was to be secured by forming an agreed panel of candidates, all standing as Sinn Féiners. Although independent candidates were to be permitted to stand, it was unclear how many would be willing to interfere in what was increasingly a two-horse race. Furthermore, after the election, a coalition cabinet would be formed, with five pro- and four anti-Treaty members, an elected President, and a Minister of Defence representing the army. The pact was entirely undemocratic, and was viewed with horror by Griffith, among many others. It was however approved at a joint meeting of the provisional government and Dáil cabinet, on the grounds that the alternative – a complete breakdown between the pro- and anti-forces – was otherwise inevitable.

The British government was, predictably, appalled at the pre-election pact. Ministers protested that, under the pact, it would be impossible for the people to freely express their opinion on the Treaty. However, an even more difficult storm was brewing, which distracted attention from the pact. Under the settlement agreed in London in 1921, the provisional government had to produce a draft constitution for the Free State before the election. This constitution had to be approved by the British government before it could go before the people, and had to reflect the key points agreed under the Treaty. Collins and Griffith had the impossible task of producing a constitution which would appease both the British and the Republicans, and their first draft, presented to the British in early June, was instantly rejected. In an attempt to keep the irregulars under control, the proposed constitution simply abandoned the oath, refused to recognise the 'special position' of Northern Ireland, and laid claim to significantly greater powers than had been agreed, specifically the right to make international treaties. Lloyd George, himself under pressure from unionists at Westminster who accused him of making concessions to terrorists, furiously insisted that the constitution be redrafted to reflect the treaty. Collins and Griffith fought hard, but reluctantly complied. The Anglo-Irish arguments meant that the new constitution was available only on the day of the election, and did not therefore achieve a wide circulation. This was to lead to accusations from the anti-Treaty camp that it had been deliberately withheld, and the public deceived into voting for a Free State which was drastically different from what they had expected. This in fact does not appear to have been the case. The people voted on the Treaty, and voted in a considerable majority in favour of it. Immediately before the election, the pact between Collins and de Valera appeared to break down. Collins made a speech in Cork at a pre-election rally in which he advised people to vote for whoever they pleased, an apparent repudiation of the pact. In fact, Collins was bowing to the inevitable. The constitution on which the country was to vote was so far from what de Valera hoped that it was impossible for the pact to survive. The despised oath was compulsory, and Ireland was to remain firmly within the Empire. His action nevertheless infuriated de Valera and his supporters, who felt that here was proof yet again that Collins was not to be trusted. In the event, the election proved a victory for the proponents of the Treaty. They won fifty-eight seats, as opposed to thirty-six for anti-Treaty candidates, while there were a surprising number of other interest group successes: labour won seventeen seats, farmers seven, and independent candidates secured ten. The strong showing by candidates not specifically linked to either the pro- or anti-Treaty sides was in itself an indication that the pact could not hold: their combined numbers almost matched the anti-Treaty camp, and they would expect a fair degree of representation. Since the labour, farmers and independent candidates were generally believed to be pro-Treaty, the result appeared an unambiguous expression of support for it, but ominously, not everybody was prepared to listen to the people.

In an unendurably tense situation, yet another drama occurred. On 22 June, Field Marshal Sir Henry Wilson, notorious for his anti-nationalist views and recently elected to the Northern Ireland Parliament, was assassinated in London by two IRA men. The British government presumed that the men were acting on orders from the IRA executive, ensconced in the Four Courts, and that the command had been given in order to scupper the fragile Anglo-Irish accord. It has been suggested that in fact the order came from Collins himself, as a response to the attacks on Catholics in Northern Ireland, but this remains speculation. It seems unlikely that Collins would have endangered the peace for which he had already sacrificed so much. The two assassins were captured, but revealed nothing of their orders before their executions on 10 August. The incident however had a significant effect upon Irish politics. The British government immediately ordered General Macready to London, and began discussing plans for an attack upon the Four Courts. Before a firm decision was made, Collins was informed in no uncertain terms that if he did not take action against O'Connor and his men, the British government would, even at the risk of uniting pro- and anti-Treaty forces against them. Without a trace of irony, the British offered to provide the necessary weaponry for an effective onslaught. Collins was once again placed in an impossible position. To be seen to act on the orders of the British, and to attack fellow Irishmen and former comrades-in-arms, would undermine his position as well as that of the new government. Not to do so meant a probable return to the Anglo-Irish War. Before crisis point was reached, however, the actions of the Four Courts garrison resolved the matter. No longer content to play a waiting game, O'Connor's men had conducted raids in Dublin, and had captured the Army Deputy Chief of Staff, J.J. O'Connell. This action convinced Collins that he must act against the garrison before they got entirely out of hand, and he decided to attack (in the event using British artillery), and the Four Courts was shelled on 28 June.

The siege of the Four Courts did not last particularly long – just two days – but it marked the irrevocable break between the pro- and anti-Treaty forces. Compromise now seemed impossible. Even those who had wavered on either side now adopted staunch positions, as each group rallied to its respective cause. Collins was faced with the urgent task of building an army – numerically the irregulars were the superior force. A massive recruitment campaign was begun, which resulted in an army of over 60,000. Many of these men were First World War veterans, already trained and experienced in warfare, significant numbers of whom had been languishing in unemployment since demobilisation. The pro-Treaty forces were therefore able to take to the field without further ado, a great advantage in this volatile situation. Although the anti-Treaty forces had apparently had the advantage, this was swiftly eroded. As F.S.L. Lyons remarked, 'as fighters they seemed to have learnt nothing and forgotten nothing', establishing themselves in buildings and locations similar to those taken, with mixed results, in the 1916 Rising. Positions were established in the city centre, with buildings apparently selected for their significance or centrality rather than ease of defence. The result was that the provisional government methodically destroyed their bases, driving them out of Dublin within eight days. The consequence of this hard line was the almost total destruction of the city centre – again – and a change in strategy for the irregulars. The original belief had been that the Dublin forces would be supplemented by brigades from around the country. This did not happen, and instead local brigades and battalions concentrated their efforts on their own areas, leading to a varied pattern of engagement with the provisional army forces. It became clear within a relatively short period of time that the anti-Treaty side had no firm plans for civil war, despite the pre-war rhetoric. There was no evidence of a plan of campaign, and the apparently random nature of their attacks alienated much of the population. Moreover there were clear disagreements within the leadership. Although de Valera had denounced the Four Courts attack, and had returned to Dublin to the Dublin Brigade battalion which he had led in 1916, he questioned the wisdom of conducting a campaign against the better equipped and growing army. He also came swiftly to the realisation that the issue would have to be resolved constitutionally, and as early as mid-July he sought to per-suade the militant irregulars to negotiate. He was singularly un-successful. Men such as Liam Lynch believed that the only solution was all-out war, and no amount of reasoned debate would convince him otherwise.

With the loss of Dublin, the majority of the anti-Treaty forces concentrated behind an imaginary line from Limerick to Waterford. Given the fact that anti-Treaty sentiment was strongest in Cork and Kerry, it was hoped that this region, jokingly known as 'the Munster Republic', could be held against the provisional government. The latter however moved swiftly to secure the large towns within and near the area, and by 20 July had taken Limerick, followed by Waterford the next day. Tipperary town was taken on 30 July, and Cashel the following day. Cork, the most important city in the 'Munster Republic', fell on 11 August to the provisional forces, who sent troops by sea. The anti-Treaty troops held no town or city of significance, and their campaign therefore shifted to a guer-rilla one, with many retreating to the mountains throughout Munster.

They were in a relatively poor position. The first phase of the civil war, described above, had brought considerable hardship to the civilian population throughout the country. The inevitable disrup-tion of transport, communications and food supplies which had occurred alienated potential supporters, and persuaded even those who had been generally sympathetic that the irregulars were acting against the wishes of the people. The loss of peace which the Treaty had promised was doubly bitter, and some of the irregu-lar forces were seen to act in a cavalier manner, bringing disruption and fear to areas which had welcomed the settlement. This is not to say that the majority were now on the side of the provisional government, but rather that its civilian opponents generally believed that constitutional opposition was the best way forward. De Valera continued to advocate this policy, arguing that the republican ideal had been admirably defended, but also that the irregulars were clearly engaged in an unwinnable war. This unwelcome advice fell on the deaf ears of the army executive. It was determined to carry on, both to ensure that the republican ideal survived, and in the lesser hope that a guerrilla campaign might achieve the same success as it had in the Anglo-Irish War. This hope was ill-founded. The troops of the provisional government were better equipped, better coordinated, and had public opinion on their side. The irregulars also faced the great difficulty of knowing that their safe houses, arms dumps and civilian supporters were all well known to men such as Collins and Mulcahy.

As the war entered its guerrilla phase, the provisional government lost its two key leaders. Arthur Griffith died of a cerebral haemorrhage on 12 August. He had been under tremendous strain, but had insisted on fulfilling all his onerous duties. Just ten days later, Michael Collins was killed at Béal na mBláth in West Cork, near to his family home. The convoy in which he was travelling was ambushed, and Collins, instead of ordering his driver to speed out of the trap, insisted on stopping to return fire. He died of a ricochet shot to the head. The loss of both men was a disaster. Although Griffith had believed in a firm line against the irregulars, Collins had continued to hope that a peace could be struck, and he was apparently on his way to a meeting with IRA leaders to discuss a settlement when he died. Collins more than anyone else understood the necessity of an agreed peace if the country was to return to some sort of normality, while Griffith believed that the irregulars should surrender unconditionally, something they absolutely refused to do. With both men dead, however, the tenor of the war changed, and for the worse.

Without the widespread support of the population, the irregulars began to adopt a strategy of ambush and sniping. The government responded with a heavy hand, and the war descended into dreadful brutality. Those suspected of ambushes or sniper attacks were likely to face summary execution or injury. The irregulars may have been clinging to a vain hope that civil war would draw Britain back into the conflict, and have the effect of uniting the warring Irish sides; if so, it was swiftly dashed. Troop withdrawals if anything became more speedy. Once it was clear that the provisional government was determined both to implement the Treaty and take a hard line with the irregulars, the British government did not interfere. On 25 August William Cosgrave was appointed head of the provisional government in Michael Collins's place, and immediately decided to tackle the war head-on. The third Dáil at last met for the first time on 9 September: although members had been elected in June, the situation in the country had made it impossible to convene an Assembly for some months. Republican members were pointedly absent, so the predominantly pro-Treaty House selected Cosgrave as President, Kevin O'Higgins as Minister for Home Affairs and Richard Mulcahy as Minister for Defence. The intentions of the new government were swiftly known. On 28 September the Dáil approved a Special Powers Bill which granted exceptional authority to the military forces in order to exercise control. The army could hold military courts to try civilians, and had the power to impose the death penalty for a wide range of offences, including the possession of weapons. The Bill signalled a determination to end the conflict quickly, but it inevitably provoked a backlash from the irregulars. They began a series of attacks upon the property and persons of those who were known to have supported the Bill, a strategy which was expanded to include those in favour of the new Dáil, especially former moderate unionists. But the irregulars found themselves under attack from another quarter. In October the Catholic Bishops issued a joint pastoral which condemned irregular activity, and attempted to force them to accept the authority of the Dáil. The pastoral declared that 'the guerrilla warfare now being carried out by the irregulars is without moral sanction, and therefore the killing of national soldiers in the course of it is murder before God.' This carried the threat of excommunication, and many irregulars were denied the sacraments by priests who believed them to be engaged in militant activity. Prisoners were routinely refused communion, and as hunger strikes became increasingly common among prisoners, they were threatened with the denial of last rites. For practising Catholics, as the vast majority of the irregulars were, this was a grievous blow, and one which created immense bitterness. What is surprising is the number of men and women who made a choice between their political convictions and their religious well-being, and denounced the Church for what they saw as its unjustified interference in matters which had nothing to do with it.

On 25 October the Dáil had approved the Constitution of the Irish Free State, and it was ratified on 5 December. Just two days later, on 7 December, the government of Northern Ireland voted to opt out of the Free State, cementing partition. Despite the best efforts of the irregulars, the new machinery of government was established, and they were under increasing pressure to abandon their campaign. In late November the Irish government, with William Cosgrave as President and Minister for Finance, Kevin O'Higgins as Vice-President and Minister for Home Affairs, Richard Mulcahy as Minister for Defence, Eoin MacNeill as Minister for Education and Ernest Blythe as Minister for Local Government, initiated a policy of execution of irregular prisoners, both for offences under their emergency powers and in reprisal for the murder of Free State government members. One of those executed was Erskine Childers, on 24 November. He had been caught in possession of a revolver, which had originally been given to him by Michael Collins. Rory O'Connor and Liam Mellows were shot, along with two others, on 8 December, in retaliation for the death of Sean Hales. By January 1923, fifty prisoners had been executed, and seventy-seven were to die in total in this way by the war's end. It was a policy which caused a serious backlash against the new Free State government, and created a sympathy for the irregulars which expressed itself in support for de Valera in the later 1920s.

The civil war was in many ways a harder fought and more bitter series of encounters than the Anglo-Irish conflict which preceded it. Certainly the 'rules of engagement' which had at least partly been observed earlier on seemed to be abandoned, and dreadful atrocities were perpetrated upon each side. The Free State troops in certain parts of the country began a policy of using irregular prisoners to clear land-mines, and there were many deaths in suspicious circumstances. The civil war divided families, and created rifts which took generations to heal. At the very moment when the country should have been working together to celebrate and secure the measure of independence won from Britain, it fractured into a series of irreconcilable interest groups. By January 1923, the Free State government had set its face against compromise, and was intent on drawing the war to as swift if inevitably bloody conclusion as possible. In early April, Liam Lynch was killed in a clash with Free State troops, thereby depriving the irregulars of their finest leader. De Valera hoped to negotiate a truce, but the government was implacable – the irregulars would surrender, or the conflict would continue. After much futile effort, de Valera finally issued a proclamation on 24 May to both the irregular forces, and his own political supporters, instructing them to cease their operations. He declared:

> Soldiers of the Republic, Legion of the Rearguard:
> The Republic can no longer be defended successfully by your arms. Further sacrifice of life would now be vain and continuance of the struggle in arms unwise in the national interest and prejudicial to the future of our cause. Military victory must be allowed to rest for the moment with those who have destroyed the Republic.

The civil war was officially over. However, the conflict continued in other forms for some time. De Valera and his followers had not surrendered, and they did not turn their weapons over to the authorities – on de Valera's instructions they either dumped them or concealed them for later use, should it become necessary. There was therefore no amnesty for known irregulars, and many, including de Valera himself, were imprisoned.

So what was the outcome of these years of conflict and open war? In the short term, the balance might appear to be negative. Ireland had not secured complete independence, the country was partitioned, and many individuals of exceptional talent had been lost. Indeed the deaths of Michael Collins, Erskine Childers, Cathal Brugha, Liam Mellows, Liam Lynch, Arthur Griffith, Harry Boland and Kevin O'Higgins (murdered in 1927) robbed the country of the leadership it so badly needed. Although they may not have shared precisely the same political convictions, these were men of great energy and commitment, who between them commanded the respect of the population. They were also, with the exceptions of Griffith and Childers, all young men, whose political careers were only just beginning. Their deaths, and the alienation of others from mainstream political life, occurred at precisely the time when the country needed firm and united leadership. In many ways, that was the real tragedy of the civil war: it sundered friendships and associations which could have made real contributions to the new Ireland, whatever shape it took, and left a legacy of bitterness from which the country took several generations to recover. The Anglo-Irish political situation deteriorated in 1925, when the long-awaited Boundary Commission singularly failed to deliver on the reforms promised to Collins and others during the Treaty debates. Relations were to further sour during the so-called Economic War in the 1930s, and as a result of Ireland's neutral stance in the Second World War (although Ireland was in fact 'neutral in favour of the allies', and forged an improved association with the British government as a result of the tacit assistance given to the war effort).

Yet it is also easy to ignore the considerable achievements of these years. With few resources, and against great odds, a measure of independence had been achieved. Although partition was to remain throughout the century, and the sectarian hatred contained within the state of Northern Ireland to erupt in a horrific manner in the 1960s and 1970s, nationalist aspirations had achieved a concrete form. The formal establishment of a Republic did not take place until 1949, when Ireland left the Commonwealth and declared the Republic, but by that stage she was, in the words of de Valera, a 'Republic in fact'. But perhaps the most important, yet most easily overlooked, result of these often confused and turbulent years was the establishment of an enduring democratic system of government. Despite its origins in the rebellion of 1916, and its consolidation in the Anglo-Irish and civil wars, the Free State and then the Republic embraced government by consent, and the precedent of political advance through violence was ignored. The Treaty may not have offered all that people hoped for, and laid the basis for a yet bloodier struggle in Northern Ireland, but it proved enough to allow the majority of the population to advance into a democratic twentieth century.

Brief biographies of principal individuals

Barton, Robert Childers (1881–1975): born Co. Wicklow; former British army officer who became Sinn Féin activist; Minister for Agriculture, 1921; initially supported the Treaty and had been one of the delegates sent to London to negotiate it, but subsequently rejected it.

Blythe, Ernest (1889–1975): born Co. Antrim; Gaelic League and IRB member, co-organiser of Irish Volunteers, 1914; Minister for Trade and Commerce, 1918–1922; supported the Treaty; played active role in Free State governments, and furthered cause of Irish theatre.

Brugha, Cathal (1874–1922): born Dublin; joined Gaelic League, 1899, and Irish Volunteers, 1913; badly wounded in 1916 Rising; IRA Chief of Staff, 1917–1919; Minister for Defence, 1919–1922; vehemently anti-Treaty; killed 7 July 1922.

Carson, Edward (1854–1935): born Dublin; called to the Irish Bar, 1889; involved in several key cases, including actions against the Plan of Campaign, 1889–1991, and the trial of Oscar Wilde, 1895; Solicitor-General, 1900–1906; leader of the Irish Unionist Party, 1910; organised unionist resistance to Home Rule; supported Larne gun-running, 1914; despite radical roles, remained at heart of government, becoming First Lord of the Admiralty, 1916, and member of the Cabinet, 1917; resigned as leader of Ulster's unionists, 1921, once Home Rule for Ulster had been abandoned.

Casement, Roger (1864–1916): born Co. Dublin; diplomat and human rights activist who reported on appalling conditions in South America and Africa; retired from diplomatic service and became active in nationalist politics; helped to fund Howth gun-running, 1914; on outbreak of First World War travelled to Germany to raise an Irish Brigade from among prisoners of war, 1914, but largely unsuccessful; returned to Ireland in 1916 in attempt to postpone the Rising, 1916; captured, tried and executed, 3 August, 1916.

Ceannt, Eamon (1881–1916): born Co. Galway; joined Gaelic League, 1900; joined Sinn Féin, 1908; founder member of the Irish Volunteers, 1913; helped coordinate Howth gun-running, 1914; signatory to the 1916 Proclamation; executed for his part in the Rising, 8 May 1916.

Childers, Erskine (1870–1922): born London; veteran of Boer War, 1899; turned to Home Rule, 1908; transported weapons in Howth gun-running, 1914; became increasingly republican during First World War; Chief Secretary to the Treaty delegation, 1921, but opposed the settlement; executed for illegal possession of a revolver during civil war, 24 November 1922.

Clarke, Thomas (1857–1916): born Isle of Wight; active in Fenian politics in the United States; imprisoned in England for dynamiting offences, 1883; emigrated to USA on his release in 1898; returned to Ireland, 1907; elected to IRB Supreme Council, 1915; fought in GPO in 1916 Rising; signatory of the Proclamation; executed, 3 May 1916.

Collins, Michael (1890–1922): born Co. Cork; worked as clerk in London; returned to Ireland, 1915; fought in GPO during 1916 Rising; Director of Intelligence during Anglo-Irish War; Minister for Home Affairs, 1918, and Minister for Finance, 1919–1922; member of Treaty delegation, 1921; prosecuted the civil war, killed in ambush, 22 August 1922.

Connolly, James (1868–1916): born Edinburgh; founded Irish Socialist Republican Party, 1896; Ulster organiser of the Irish Transport and General Workers' Union, 1910; active in trade union organisation in Dublin, and coordinated worker resistance in the 1913 lock-out; founded the Irish Citizen Army as response to police brutality against workers, 1913; fought in the GPO in 1916 Rising; co-author and signatory of the Proclamation of the Irish Republic, April 1916; executed for his part in the Rising, 12 May 1916.

Cosgrave, William Thomas (1880–1965): born Dublin; joined Irish Volunteers, 1913; fought in 1916 Rising; Minister for Local Government in first Dáil; supported the Treaty; President of

second Dáil and Chairman of the provisional government following deaths of Griffith and Collins; Minister of Finance, 1922–
1923; took tough line against anti-Treaty forces in civil war;
remained politically active until retirement in 1944.

Craig, James (1871–1940): born Belfast; veteran of Anglo-Boer
War, 1900–1901; unionist MP for various Ulster constituencies,
1906–1918; Orange Order officer and held governmental secre-
taryships, 1919–1921; replaced Carson as leader of the Ulster
Unionist Party, 1921; first Prime Minister of Northern Ireland,
1921.

Davitt, Michael (1846–1906): born Co. Mayo; Fenian activist,
founded Land League of Mayo in 1878, and National Land
League in 1879; helped organise Ladies' Land League, 1880;
joined anti-Parnellite faction after Irish Parliamentary Party split.

De Valera, Eamon (1882–1975): born New York; returned to
Ireland as young child; joined Gaelic League, 1908; joined Irish
Volunteers, 1913; fought in 1916 Rising, death sentence com-
muted because of American citizenship; President of Sinn Féin,
1917–1926; President of first Dáil Éireann, 1919; fund-raised in
USA, 1919–1920; President of the Irish Republic, 1921; opposed
Treaty, 1921; founded Cumann na Poblachta, 1922; sidelined in
civil war, but returned to mainstream politics with the creation of
Fianna Fáil, 1926; dominated Irish political life as Taoiseach and
President until his death.

Gonne, Maud [MacBride] (1866–1953): born Aldershot, England;
founded Inghinidhe na hÉireann, 1900; active in French as well
as Irish radical politics, 1880 onwards; played the lead in *Cathleen
ni Houlihan*, 1902, confirming her place both as Yeats's muse and
the personification of Irish nationalist aspiration; separated from
her husband John MacBride in 1905, and lived in Paris, fearing
that she would lose her son to her husband's family if she returned
to Ireland; finally returned in 1917 after MacBride's execution in
1916; active in republican prisoners' associations before and after
the civil war.

Gregory, Isabella Augusta (née Persse, 1852–1932): born Co.
Galway; co-founder of the Irish Literary Theatre, 1898; author
of over forty plays; patronised Irish literary talent including
Sean O'Casey and John Millington Synge, and most notably
William Butler Yeats, with whom she co-wrote several plays;
director of the Abbey Theatre Company, 1904–1928.

Griffith, Arthur (1871–1922): born Dublin; radical, although not militant, nationalist; Gaelic League and IRB member, founded Cumann na nGaedheal, 1900; proposed that Ireland should look to the Hungarian example of dual monarchy as a model for Ireland, 1904; founded Sinn Féin, 1908; joined Irish Volunteers, 1913; imprisoned twice, 1916–1918; President of the Dáil, 1919; leader of the Irish delegation during the Treaty debates, 1921; President of the Dáil, 1922.

Healy, Timothy Michael (1855–1931): born Co. Cork; MP and lawyer, led the anti-Parnellite Irish National Federation following the Parnell split in the Irish Parliamentary Party; rejoined the IPP in 1900 but was expelled two years later; Governor-General of the Irish Free State, 1922–1928.

Hobson, Bulmer (1883–1969): born Belfast; joined Gaelic League, 1901; founded Fianna Éireann, 1903; joined IRB, 1904; co-founded Dungannon Clubs, 1905; Vice-President of Sinn Féin, 1907; Secretary of the Irish Volunteers, 1913, and co-ordinated the Howth gun-running, 1914; withdrew from militant bodies, 1914.

Hyde, Douglas (1860–1947): born Sligo; co-founder of the Irish Literary Society in 1891; President of the National Literary Society, 1892; delivered his lecture 'The Necessity of De-Anglicizing Ireland', 1892 (published 1894); co-founder and President of the Gaelic League, 1893, from which he resigned in 1915 because he feared it was becoming too politicised; President of the Irish Republic, 1938.

Larkin, James (1876–1947): born Liverpool; labour activist, organised several strikes in Belfast and Dublin, 1907; encouraged workers to organise into trade unions, established the Irish Transport and General Workers' Union, 1908; President of the Irish Trades Union Congress, 1911; coordinated Dublin workers in 1913 lock-out; occupied with trade union activities in the United States, 1914–1923; returned to Ireland 1923, to find much of his support eroded.

Lynch, Liam (1893–1923): born Co. Limerick; active in Volunteers; fought in Anglo-Irish War; opposed the Treaty; eventually joined the occupying garrison in the Four Courts in June 1922; conducted campaign against Free State forces, 1922–1923; fatally wounded, 10 April 1923.

MacDermott, Sean (1884–1916): born Co. Leitrim; joined Gaelic League and IRB, 1906; despite physical difficulties caused by polio, 1912, was active in Volunteers; planned the 1916 Rising, and fought in GPO; signatory of the 1916 Proclamation; executed, 12 May 1916.

MacDonagh, Thomas (1878–1916): born Co. Tipperary; joined Gaelic League, 1901; assisted Patrick Pearse in establishment of St Enda's school, 1908; founder member of the Irish Volunteers, 1913; joined IRB, 1915; signatory to the 1916 Proclamation; executed for his part in the Rising, 3 May 1916.

MacNeill, Eoin (1867–1945): born Co. Antrim; Vice-President of Gaelic League, 1893; Chief of Staff of Irish Volunteers; not informed about 1916 Rising until shortly before it was due to take place; countermanded Pearse's orders to the Volunteers; Minister of Finance in First Dáil, 1919; Minister for Industries, 1919–1921; supported the Treaty; Minister of Education, 1922–1925; Free State representative on Boundary Commission, but resigned in protest over its lack of effectiveness.

MacSwiney, Terence (1879–1920): born Cork; Gaelic Revival activist and author of plays and poetry; co-founder of Cork Volunteers, 1913; elected to first Dáil for West Cork, 1919; active in Dáil arbitration courts; Lord Mayor of Cork, 1920; arrested August 1920; died Brixton Prison, 25 October 1920, after 74-day hunger strike.

Markievicz, Constance (née Gore-Booth, 1868–1927): born London; despite Ascendancy background, became active in nationalist politics, joined Sinn Féin, 1909; joined Inghinidhe na hÉireann; officer of the Irish Citizen Army, with whom she fought in the 1916 Rising; sentenced to death for her part, but commuted to life imprisonment on grounds of sex; President of Cumann na mBan, 1917; first woman to be elected to House of Commons, but did not take seat, 1918; Minister for Labour, 1919–1921; rejected Treaty.

Mellows, Liam (1892–1922) born Lancashire; joined IRB, 1912; founder member of Irish Volunteers, 1913; fought in 1916 Rising; IRA Director of Purchases, 1921, opposed the Treaty; occupied the Four Courts, 1922; executed, 8 December 1922.

Mulcahy, Richard (1886–1971): born Waterford; joined Irish Volunteers, 1913; fought in 1916 Rising; IRA Chief of Staff, supported the Treaty; commanded the provisional government's military forces, 1922–1923; had distinguished political career in Free State and Irish Republic.

O'Connor, Rory (1883–1922): born Dublin; fought in 1916 Rising; rejected the Treaty; led the occupation of the Four Courts in April 1922; surrendered, June 1922; executed, 8 December 1922.

O'Higgins, Kevin (1892–1927): born Co. Laois; Sinn Féin activist; Assistant Minister for Local Government in 1919 Dáil; pro-Treaty; Minister for Economic Affairs, 1922; Minister for Justice and External Affairs, 1922–1927; was responsible for taking a firm line in order to end the civil war; killed by IRA gunman, 10 July 1927.

O'Malley, Ernest (1898–1957): born Co. Mayo; joined Irish Volunteers, 1917; IRA member, 1919, and active in Anglo-Irish War; rejected Treaty, 1921; fought in civil war, wounded and imprisoned, 1922; released, 1924.

O'Rahilly, Michael Joseph [The O'Rahilly] (1875–1916): born Co. Kerry; active in Gaelic League and Sinn Féin; participated in Howth gun-running, 1914; believed Rising was doomed to failure, but participated nevertheless; fatally wounded during evacuation of GPO.

Parnell, Anna (1852–1911): born Co. Wicklow; sister of Charles Stewart; began political activism through famine relief work; established Ladies' Land League, 1881; coordinated tenant resistance in line with stated Land League policy, 1881–1882; clashed with C.S. Parnell and other Land League leaders, 1882; withdrew from active participation in Irish politics, 1882.

Parnell, Charles Stewart (1846–1891): born Co. Wicklow; landowner, MP for Meath, 1875; President of the Land League, 1879; Leader of the Irish Parliamentary Party, 1880; championed Home Rule cause; cited as co-respondent in divorce case of Katharine O'Shea, which lost support of political allies; married O'Shea in 1891 shortly before his death.

Pearse, Patrick (1879–1916): born Dublin; lawyer, educationalist, rebel; joined Gaelic League, 1896; editor of *An Claidheamh Soluis* 1903–1909; founded St Enda's Irish language school, 1908; founder member of Irish Volunteers; delivered oration at O'Donovan Rossa's funeral, 1915; delivered Proclamation of Independence during the Easter Rising, 1916; executed, 3 May 1916.

Plunkett, Joseph Mary (1887–1916): born Dublin; poet and rebel, joined IRB, 1913; organiser, Irish Volunteers, 1913; worked with Casement in securing arms from Germany, 1915; played little active part in 1916 Rising because of severe illness, but was signatory to Proclamation; married Grace Gifford in Kilmainham Gaol on eve of his execution, 3 May 1916.

Redmond, John (1856–1918): born Co. Wexford; MP for various constituencies, 1881–1918; leader of the Parnellite section of the Irish Parliamentary Party following the split in 1891; reunited the Party, 1900; worked tirelessly for Home Rule, securing such a bill in 1914 (suspended for the duration of the war); devastated by the 1916 Rising, and loss of his brother in the war.

Sheehy Skeffington, Francis (1878–1916): born Co. Cavan; resigned post as Registrar of University College, Dublin, in protest against the restrictions upon women in higher education; married Hanna Sheehy, 1903, and added her surname to his; active in nationalist politics, but a committed pacifist, resigned from the Irish Citizen Army when it committed itself to militantism; campaigned against recruitment; arrested while trying to prevent looting during the 1916 Rising, and summarily executed, 26 April 1916.

Sheehy Skeffington, Hanna (1877–1946): born Co. Tipperary; feminist nationalist who, on her marriage to Francis Skeffington, added his name to hers, as he also did; co-founder of Irish Women's Franchise League, 1908; pressurised Redmond unsuccessfully to include a votes for women clause in any Home Rule bill; husband murdered by crown forces during 1916 Rising, she refused £10,000 in compensation for his death, and insisted on official enquiry; public speaker on Irish situation in United States, 1916–1918; rejected Treaty.

Yeats, William Butler (1865–1939): born Dublin; foremost figure of the Irish literary revival; author of *The Countess Cathleen* (1899) and *Cathleen ni Houlihan* (1902), co-founder of the Abbey Theatre, 1904; gradually became disillusioned with radical nationalism; Free State Senator, 1922–1928, and a vocal defender of the Anglo-Irish tradition; Nobel Prize for Literature, 1923.

Select further reading

Andrews, C.S. *Dublin Made Me* (Cork, 1979).

Augusteijn, Joost *From Public Defiance to Guerrilla Warfare: The Experience of Ordinary Volunteers in the Irish War of Independence, 1916–1921* (Dublin, 1996).

Bardon, Jonathan *A History of Ulster* (Belfast, 1992).

Barry, Tom *Guerrilla Days in Ireland* (Dublin, 1949).

Bartlett, Thomas and Jeffery, Keith *A Military History of Ireland* (Cambridge, 1996).

Beckett, J.C. *The Making of Modern Ireland, 1603–1923* (London, 1966).

Beckett, J.C. *The Anglo-Irish Tradition* (London, 1976).

Bell, J. Bowyer *The Secret Army: A History of the Irish Republican Army, 1916–1970* (London, 1970).

Bence-Jones, Mark *Twilight of the Ascendancy* (London, 1987).

Bennett, Richard *The Black and Tans* (London, 1959).

Bew, Paul *Land and the National Question, 1858–82* (Dublin, 1979).

Bew, Paul *Conflict and Conciliation in Ireland, 1890–1910: Parnellites and Agrarian Radicals* (Oxford, 1987).

Bew, Paul *Ideology and the Irish Question: Ulster Unionism and Irish Nationalism, 1912–1916* (Oxford, 1994).

Bowen, Kurt *Protestants in a Catholic State: Ireland's Privileged Minority* (Montreal, 1983).

Boyce, D. George *Englishmen and Irish Troubles: British Public Opinion and the Making of Irish Policy, 1918–1922* (London, 1972).

Boyce, D. George *Nationalism in Ireland* (London, 1982).

Boyce, D. George *Nineteenth-Century Ireland: The Search for Stability* (Dublin, 1990).

Boyce, D. George and O'Day, Alan (eds) *Parnell in Perspective* (London, 1991).

Breen, Dan *My Fight for Irish Freedom* (Dublin, 1924)

Brown, Terence *Ireland: A Social and Cultural History, 1922–1979* (London, 1981).

Buckland, Patrick *Irish Unionism I: The Anglo-Irish and the New Ireland, 1885–1922* (Dublin, 1972).

Buckland, Patrick *Irish Unionism II: Ulster Unionism and the Origins of Northern Ireland, 1886–1922* (Dublin, 1973).

Bull, Philip *Land, Politics and Nationalism: A Study of the Irish Land Question* (Dublin, 1996).

Callanan, Frank *The Parnell Split, 1890–91* (Cork, 1992).

Campbell, Colm *Emergency Law in Ireland, 1918–25* (Oxford, 1994).

Canning, Paul *British Policy Towards Ireland, 1921–41* (Oxford, 1985).

Clarke, Kathleen *Revolutionary Woman: An Autobiography, 1878–1972* (Dublin, 1991).

Collins, Peter (ed.) *Nationalism and Unionism: Conflict in Ireland, 1885–1921* (Belfast, 1994).

Comerford, R.V. *The Fenians in Context: Irish Politics and Society, 1848–1882* (Dublin, 1985).

Conlon, Lil *Cumann na mBan and the Women of Ireland, 1913–1925* (Kilkenny, 1969).

Coogan, Tim Pat *Michael Collins: A Biography* (London, 1990).

Coogan, Tim Pat *De Valera: Long Fellow, Long Shadow* (London, 1993).

Costello, Francis J. *Enduring the Most: The Life and Death of Terence MacSwiney* (Dingle, 1995).

Cote, Jane McL. *Fanny and Anna Parnell: Ireland's Patriot Sisters* (London, 1991).

Coulter, Carol *The Hidden Tradition: Feminism, Women and Nationalism in Ireland* (Cork, 1993).

Coxhead, Elizabeth *Daughters of Erin: Five Women of the Irish Renaissance* (London, 1965).

Cronin, Sean *Irish Nationalism* (Dublin, 1980).

Curran, Joseph M. *The Birth of the Irish Free State, 1921–1923* (Alabama, 1980).

Curtis, L.P. *Coercion and Conciliation in Ireland, 1880–1892: A Study in Conservative Unionism* (Princeton, 1963).

Daly, Mary E. *Social and Economic History of Ireland since 1800* (Dublin, 1981).

Daly, Mary E. *Dublin, The Deposed Capital: A Social and Economic History, 1860–1914* (Cork, 1985).

Dangerfield, George *The Damnable Question: A Study in Anglo-Irish Relations* (London, 1979).

Davis, Richard *Arthur Griffith and Non-Violent Sinn Fein* (Dublin, 1974).

De Búrca, Marcus *The GAA: A History* (Dublin, 1980).

Deasy, Liam *Towards Ireland Free* (Cork, 1973).

Dunleavy, Janet Egleson and Dunleavy, Gareth W. *Douglas Hyde: A Maker of Modern Ireland* (Berkeley, 1991).

Dwyer, T. Ryle *Eamon de Valera* (Dublin, 1980).

Edwards, Ruth Dudley *Patrick Pearse: The Triumph of Failure* (London, 1977).

English, Richard *Ernie O'Malley: IRA Intellectual* (Oxford, 1998).

Farrell, Brian *The Founding of Dáil Éireann: Parliament and Nation-Building* (Dublin, 1971).

Farrell, Michael *Arming the Protestants: The Formation of the Ulster Special Constabulary and the Royal Ulster Constabulary, 1920–27* (London, 1983).

Fitzpatrick, David *Politics and Irish Life, 1913–21: Provincial Experience of War and Revolution* (Dublin, 1977).

Fitzpatrick, David *Irish Emigration, 1801–1921* (Dundalk, 1984).

Fitzpatrick, David *The Two Irelands, 1912–1939* (Oxford, 1998).

Follis, Bryan A. *A State Under Siege: The Establishment of Northern Ireland, 1920–1925* (Oxford, 1995).

Foster, R.F. *Charles Stewart Parnell: The Man and His Family* (Hassocks, 1976).

Foster, R.F. *Modern Ireland, 1600–1972* (London, 1988).

Foster, R.F. *Paddy and Mr Punch: Connections in Irish and English History* (London, 1993).

Foster, R.F. *W.B. Yeats: A Life. I: The Apprentice Mage* (Oxford, 1997).

Gailey, Andrew *Ireland and the Death of Kindness: The Experience of Constructive Unionism, 1890–1905* (Cork, 1987).

Gallagher, Frank *The Indivisible Island: The History of the Partition of Ireland* (London, 1957).

Garvin, Tom *The Evolution of Irish Nationalist Politics* (Dublin, 1981).

Garvin, Tom *Nationalist Revolutionaries in Ireland, 1858–1928* (Oxford, 1987).

Garvin, Tom *1922: The Birth of Irish Democracy* (Dublin, 1996).

Gray, John *City in Revolt: James Larkin and the Belfast Dock Strike of 1907* (Belfast, 1985).

Greaves, C. Desmond *The Life and Times of James Connolly* (London, 1961).

Greaves, C. Desmond *The Irish Transport and General Workers' Union: The Formative Years, 1909–1923* (Dublin, 1982).

Harkness, David *Ireland in the Twentieth Century: Divided Island* (London, 1996).

Harris, Mary *The Catholic Church and the Foundation of the Northern Irish State* (Cork, 1993).

Haverty, Anne *Constance Markievicz* (London, 1988).

Hennessey, Thomas *A History of Northern Ireland, 1920–1996* (Dublin, 1997).

Holmes, Janice and Urquhart, Diane (eds) *Coming into the Light: The Work, Politics and Religion of Women in Ulster, 1840–1940* (Belfast, 1994).

Hopkinson, Michael *Green Against Green: The Irish Civil War* (Dublin, 1988).

Hoppen, K. Theodore *Ireland Since 1800: Conflict and Conformity* (London, 1989).

Hume, David *For Ulster and Her Freedom: The Story of the April 1914 Gunrunning* (Lurgan, 1989).

Hutchinson, John *The Dynamics of Cultural Nationalism: The Gaelic Revival and the Creation of the Irish Nation State* (London, 1987).

Innes, C.L. *Women and Nation in Irish Literature and Society, 1800–1935* (Hemel Hempstead, 1993).

Jackson, Alvin *The Ulster Party: Irish Unionists in the House of Commons, 1884–1911* (Oxford, 1989).

Jackson, Alvin *Sir Edward Carson* (Dublin, 1993).

Jackson, Alvin *Ireland 1798–1998: Politics and War* (Oxford, 1999).

Jalland, Patricia *The Liberals and Ireland: The Ulster Question in British Politics to 1914* (Brighton, 1980).

Jones, Mary *These Obstreperous Lassies: A History of the Irish Women Workers' Union* (Dublin, 1988).

Kee, Robert *The Laurel and the Ivy: The Story of Charles Stewart Parnell and Irish Nationalism* (London, 1993).

Keogh, Dermot *Twentieth-Century Ireland: Nation and State* (Dublin, 1994).

Kiberd, Declan *Inventing Ireland: The Literature of the Modern Nation* (London, 1995).

Kiely, David M. *John Millington Synge: A Biography* (Dublin, 1994).

Kingham, Nancy *United We Stood: The Story of the Ulster Women's Unionist Council, 1911–1974* (Belfast, 1975).

Kotsonouris, Mary *Retreat From Revolution: The Dáil Courts, 1920–24* (Dublin, 1995).

Laffan, Michael *The Partition of Ireland, 1911–1925* (Dundalk, 1983).

Larkin, Emmet *James Larkin: Irish Labour Leader, 1876–1947* (London, 1965).

Lawlor, Sheila *Britain and Ireland, 1914–23* (Dublin, 1983).

Lee, J.J. *The Modernisation of Irish Society, 1848–1914* (Dublin, 1973).

Lee, J.J. *Ireland, 1912–1985* (Cambridge, 1989).

Levenson, Leah and Natterstad, Jerry H. *Hanna Sheehy Skeffington, Irish Feminist* (Syracuse, 1986).

Linklater, Andro *An Unhusbanded Life. Charlotte Despard: Suffragette, Socialist and Sinn Féiner* (London, 1980).

Loughlin, James *Gladstone, Home Rule and the Ulster Question, 1882–93* (Dublin, 1986).

Loughlin, James *Ulster Unionism and British National Identity since 1885* (London, 1995).

Luddy, Maria *Hanna Sheehy Skeffington* (Dublin, 1995).

Luddy, Maria *Women in Ireland, 1900–18: A Documentary History* (Cork, 1995).

Luddy, Maria and Murphy, Cliona (eds) *Women Surviving: Studies in Irish Women's History in the 19th and 20th Centuries* (Swords, 1990).

Lyons, F.S.L. *The Fall of Parnell, 1890–91* (London, 1960).

Lyons, F.S.L. *Ireland Since the Famine* (London, 1971).

Lyons, F.S.L. *Culture and Anarchy in Ireland, 1890–1939* (Oxford, 1979).

McBride, Lawrence W. *The Greening of Dublin Castle: The Transformation of Bureaucratic and Judicial Personnel in Ireland, 1892–1922* (Washington, 1991).

McCartney, Donal (ed.) *Parnell: The Politics of Power* (Dublin, 1991).

McColgan, John *British Policy and the Irish Administration, 1920–1922* (London, 1983).

MacCurtain, Margaret and Ó Corráin, Donncha (eds) *Women in Irish Society: The Historical Dimension* (Dublin, 1978).

MacDonagh, Oliver *Ireland: The Union and its Aftermath* (London, 1977).

MacDonagh, Oliver *States of Mind: A Study of Anglo-Irish Conflict, 1780–1980* (London, 1983).

MacDonagh, Oliver *O'Connell: The Life of Daniel O'Connell, 1775–1847* (London, 1991).

McDowell, R.B. *The Irish Administration, 1801–1914* (London, 1964).

McDowell, R.B. *The Irish Convention, 1917–18* (London, 1970).

McDowell, R.B. *The Church of Ireland, 1869–1969* (London, 1975).

Macmillan, Gretchen *State, Society and Authority in Ireland: The Foundations of the Modern State* (Dublin, 1993).

Maher, Jim *The Flying Column: West Kilkenny, 1916–21* (Dublin, 1987).

Mandle, W.F. *The Gaelic Athletic Association and Irish Nationalist Politics, 1884–1924* (London, 1987).

Mansergh, Nicholas *The Unresolved Question: The Anglo-Irish Settlement and its Undoing, 1912–1972* (New Haven, 1991).

Martin, F.X. (ed.) *Leaders and Men of the 1916 Rising: Dublin, 1916* (London, 1967).

Matthew, H.C.G. *Gladstone 1875–1898* (Oxford, 1995).

Maye, Brian *Arthur Griffith* (Dublin, 1997).

Miller, David W. *Church, State and Nation in Ireland, 1898–1921* (Dublin, 1973).

Miller, David W. *Queen's Rebels: Ulster Loyalism in Historical Perspective* (Dublin, 1978).

Mitchell, Arthur *Labour in Irish Politics, 1890–1930: The Irish Labour Movement in an Age of Revolution* (Dublin, 1974).

Mitchell, Arthur *Revolutionary Government in Ireland: Dáil Éireann, 1919–22* (Dublin, 1995).

Moody, T.W. (ed.) *The Fenian Movement* (Cork, 1968).

Morgan, Austen *Labour and Partition: The Belfast Working Class, 1905–23* (London, 1991).

Mulvihill, Margaret *Charlotte Despard: A Biography* (London, 1989).

Murphy, Brian P. *Patrick Pearse and the Lost Republican Ideal* (Dublin, 1991).

Murphy, Cliona *The Women's Suffrage Movement and Irish Society in the Early Twentieth Century* (Hemel Hempstead, 1989).

Murphy, John A. *Ireland in the Twentieth Century* (Dublin, 1975).

Neeson, Eoin *Birth of a Republic: The Republican Thrust for Liberty in Ireland, 1798–1923* (Dublin, 1998).

Ní Dhonnchadha, Máirín and Dorgan, Theo (eds) *Revising the Rising* (Derry, 1991).

Norman, Diana *Terrible Beauty: A Life of Constance Markievicz, 1868–1927* (London, 1987).

Nowlan, Kevin B. *The Making of 1916: Studies in the History of the Rising* (Dublin, 1969).

O'Brien, Conor Cruise *Parnell and His Party, 1880–90* (Oxford, 1957).

O'Broin, Leon *Dublin Castle and the 1916 Rising* (London, 1966).

O'Broin, Leon *Revolutionary Underground: The Story of the Irish Republican Brotherhood, 1858–1924* (Dublin, 1976).

O'Connor, Emmet *A Labour History of Ireland, 1924–1960* (Dublin, 1992).

O'Day, Alan *The English Face of Irish Nationalism: Parnellite Involvement in British Politics, 1880–86* (Hampshire, 1994).

O'Day, Alan *Charles Stewart Parnell* (Dublin, 1998).

O'Day, Alan *Irish Home Rule, 1867–1921* (Manchester, 1998).

O'Farrell, Patrick *Ireland's English Question: Anglo-Irish Relations, 1534–1970* (London, 1971).

O'Farrell, Patrick *England and Ireland Since 1800* (Oxford, 1975).

Ó Gráda, Cormac *A New Economic History of Ireland, 1780–1939* (Oxford, 1994).

O'Halpin, Eunan *The Decline of the Union: British Government in Ireland, 1892–1920* (Dublin, 1987).

O'Neill, Marie *From Parnell to de Valera: A Biography of Jennie Wyse Power, 1858–1941* (Dublin, 1991).

Orr, Philip *The Road to the Somme: Men of the Ulster Division Tell Their Story* (Belfast, 1987).

Owens, Rosemary Cullen *Smashing Times: A History of the Irish Women's Suffrage Movement, 1889–1922* (Dublin, 1984).

Phoenix, Eamon *Northern Nationalism: Nationalist Politics, Partition and the Catholic Minority in Northern Ireland, 1890–1940* (Belfast, 1994).

Ryan, A.P. *Mutiny at the Curragh* (London, 1956).

Shannon, Catherine B. *Arthur J. Balfour and Ireland, 1874–1922* (Washington, 1988).

Sheehy, Jeanne *The Rediscovery of Ireland's Past: The Celtic Revival, 1830–1930* (London, 1980).

Solow, Barbara *The Land Question and the Irish Economy, 1870–1903* (Cambridge, Mass., 1974).

Stewart, A.T.Q. *The Ulster Crisis: Resistance to Home Rule, 1912–14* (London, 1967).

Stewart, A.T.Q. *Edward Carson* (Dublin, 1981).

Thompson, D.I. *The Imagination of an Insurrection: Dublin, Easter 1916* (New York, 1967).

Townshend, Charles *The British Campaign in Ireland, 1919–1921: The Development of Political and Military Policies* (Oxford, 1975).

Townshend, Charles *Political Violence in Ireland: Government and Resistance since 1848* (Oxford, 1983).

Travers, Pauric *Settlements and Divisions: Ireland, 1870–1922* (Dublin, 1988).

Urquhart, Diane *Women in Ulster Politics, 1890–1940* (Dublin, 2000).

Valiulis, Maryann Gialanella *Portrait of a Revolutionary: General Richard Mulcahy and the Foundation of the Irish Free State* (Dublin, 1992).

Van Voris, Jacqueline *Constance de Markievicz: In the Cause of Ireland* (Amherst, 1967).

Vaughan, W.E. (ed.) *A New History of Ireland V: Ireland Under the Union I: 1801–1870* (Oxford, 1989).

Vaughan, W.E. (ed.) *A New History of Ireland V: Ireland Under the Union II: 1870–1921* (Oxford, 1996).

Ward, Margaret *Unmanageable Revolutionaries: Women and Irish Nationalism* (London, 1983).

Ward, Margaret *Maud Gonne: Ireland's Joan of Arc* (London, 1990).

Ward, Margaret *Hanna Sheehy Skeffington: A Life* (Cork, 1997).

Watson, George J. *Irish Identity and the Literary Revival* (London, 1979).

West, Trevor *Horace Plunkett: Cooperation and Politics: An Irish Biography* (Gerrards Cross, 1986).

Whyte, J. H. *Church and State in Modern Ireland, 1923–1979* (Dublin, 1980).

Younger, Calton *Ireland's Civil War* (London, 1968).

Index

Aberdeen, Lady 23–4
Act of Union 1800 1
agriculture 3–4, 5; *see also* land
American Commission on
 Conditions in Ireland 68
An Claidheamh Soluis (Sword of
 Light) 38
Anglo-Boer War 26
Anglo-Irish War 57–73
anti-Treaty IRA 92–3, 94, 96–102
arms shipments 38, 39–40, 44
Army Document 94
Ashbourne Purchase Act 1885 17
Asquith, H.H. 51
Aud 44–5
Auxiliary Division 66–7

Bachelor's Walk incident 40
Balfour, Gerald 27
Barry, Tom 49, 76
Barton, Robert 59, 77, 78, 79, 85,
 104
Belfast 90
Belfast Boycott 69
Birkenhead, Lord 79
Black and Tans 66–7, 70
'Bloody Sunday' 70–1
Blythe, Ernest 89, 101, 104
Boland, Harry 102
'Book of Kells' 13
Boundary Commission 81, 82, 83,
 90, 103
Bowen-Colthurst, Captain 47–8

boycotts 11, 69
Breen, Dan 61
British Army, Irishmen in 48–50
British Commonwealth 81
British intelligence agents 64–5, 70
Brugha, Cathal 56, 58, 59, 78, 94,
 102, 104; and IRA 62–3;
 legitimate targets 65; and Treaty
 85
Burke, T.H. 14
Butler, Maire 31
Butt, Isaac 10

Canada 84
Carson, Edward 37–8, 41, 104
Casement, Roger 40, 44, 104–5
Cathleen ni Houlihan (Yeats and
 Gregory) 21
Catholic Association 3
Catholic Bishops' pastoral 100
Catholic Church 2, 34, 36
Catholic Emancipation 3
Catholics, attacks on 90
Cavendish, Lord F. 14
Ceannt, E. 43, 46, 51, 105
Celtic Revival 18–21, 22
Chamberlain, Austen 79
Chamberlain, Joseph 16
Childers, Erskine 40, 77, 82, 101,
 102, 105
Church of Ireland 2, 14
Churchill, Winston 79
City Hall 45–6

Civil Authorities (Special Powers)
Bill 91
Civil Service 92
Civil War 89–103
Clancy, Peadar 71
Clarke, Kathleen 86
Clarke, Tom 35, 44, 46, 51, 105
Cohalan, Judge, D. 64
Colbert, Con 51
Collins, Michael 36, 50, 56, 58,
72, 78, 102, 105; agreement
with Craig 90–1; Civil War 93;
Dail Éireann National Loan 60;
Four Courts 96–7; intelligence
officers 64–5, 70; killed by
ambush 99; military campaign
62–3; pre-election pact 94, 95–6;
provisional government 89–90,
91–2; second Dáil 59; Sinn Féin
funds 64–5; Treaty 76–7, 79,
83–4, 85–6, 87, 88
compulsory land purchase 25, 26
Congested Districts Board 26–7
Connolly, James 31–2, 34–5, 105;
Easter Rising 43, 44, 45, 46, 47,
51
conscription 54–6
Conservative and Unionist
Women's Suffrage Association 30
constitutional position 80–2
cooperative campaign 24
Cork 71, 98
Cosgrave, W.T. 59, 78, 85, 89,
100, 101, 105–6
cottiers 3, 4, 5
courts 60–1
Craig, James 38, 72, 80, 82, 83,
106; agreement with Collins
90–1; six counties 76, 81
Criminal Law Amendment Act
1887 17
crown, Ireland's relationship to
80–2
culture 18–23
Cumann na mBan (Council of
Irishwomen) 29–30, 43, 47, 65,
87, 92

Cumann na nGaedheal 30–1
Cumann na Poblachta (League of
the Republic) 93, 94
Curragh Incident 38
Cusack, M. 18

Dáil Courts 60–1
Dáil Éireann 94, 95; first meeting
58–9; second meeting 59–60;
third meeting 100; Treaty of
1921 74–88
Dáil Éireann National Loan 60
Daly, Edward 51
Davis, Thomas 6
Davitt, Michael 10, 12, 106
De Valera, Eamon 62–3, 76–7,
103, 106; Civil War 93–4, 98,
99, 102; Document No. 2 86,
87; Easter Rising 1916 46, 51;
escape from prison 59; Oath of
Allegiance 82, 87; pre-election
pact 94, 95–6; President of the
Irish Republic 77; resignation
from Presidency 88; rise of
Sinn Féin 52–3; Treaty 76–9,
85, 87; truce 72–3; visit to US
64
Deasy, Liam 76
Defence of the Realm Amendment
Act 1915 50
Democratic Programme 59
Department of Agriculture and
Technical Instruction 27
Despard, Charlotte 65
Devoy, John 64
Dillon, John Blake 6, 17
Dillon, John 51, 53, 55
Document No. 2 86, 87
Dominion status 77, 83, 84–5
draft constitution for the Free State
90, 95
Dublin: Civil War 97–8; Easter
1916 45–50
Dublin Castle 45, 92
Dublin Metropolitan Police Force
34
Duffy, Charles Gavan 6, 7

Nathan, Sir Matthew 44
Nation 6
National Council 31
National Land League 10–11
National Literary Society 22
National Repeal Association 6–7
National Volunteers 41, 49
nationalism 20, 23, 35–6, 38–40
'No Rent' Manifesto 13
Northern Ireland government 72, 90–1, 94, 101

Oath of Allegiance to the crown 82, 83, 87
O'Brien, William 17, 25, 26
O'Casey, Sean 21
O'Connell, Daniel 2–3, 6
O'Connell, J.J. 97
O'Connor, Rory 92, 93, 94, 96–7, 101, 109
O'Farrell, Elizabeth 50
Óglaigh na hÉireann *see* Irish Republican Army
O'Hanrahan, Michael 51
O'Higgins, Kevin 89, 100, 101, 102, 109
O'Malley, Ernie 88, 92, 109
O'Rahilly, The (M.J.) 39, 41, 110
organised labour 31–5
O'Shea, Captain 18
O'Shea, Katharine 17–18

Parliament Act 1911 28
Parnell, Anna 12, 13, 14, 109
Parnell, Charles Stewart 9–12, 13–14, 17–18, 25, 109
Parnell, Fanny 12
partition 81, 85, 86, 103
peace negotiations 78–85
Pearse, Margaret 86
Pearse, Patrick 36, 41, 109; Easter Rising 43, 46, 50, 51
Pearse, William 51
Peel, Sir Robert 4
Penal Laws 2
People's Rights Association 26
Phoenix Park murders 14

Plunkett, Count George Noble 52, 58, 59
Plunkett, Sir Horace 24
Plunkett, Joseph Mary 41, 43, 46, 47, 51, 109
police 91
potato 3–4
Power, Jenny Wyse 29
pre-election pact 94–5, 95–6
provisional government: Easter Rising 46; 1922 89–90, 94, 95, 97–8, 99
Plan of Campaign 17, 38

radicalism 6
railway strike 61
rebellions: 1798 1; 1803 1; 1848 7; *see also* Easter Rising 1916
reciprocal citizenship 80
recruitment 97
Redmond, John 30, 49, 53, 54–5, 110; Irish Parliamentary Party 25, 26, 27–8; Irish Volunteers 39, 40–1
religion 5–6; *see also* Church of Ireland; Roman Catholicism
rent strikes 12, 13
rents, regulation of 11–12
Republican Bonds 64
Restoration of Order In Ireland Act 69–70
Rice, Mary Spring 40
Rising of 1916 31, 34, 42–56
Robinson, Seamus 61
Roman Catholic Relief Act 1829 3
Roman Catholicism 2, 3, 34, 36
Royal Irish Constabulary (RIC) 61–2, 64, 65–6, 68
Royal Ulster Constabulary 91
Russell, Lord John 4

Salisbury, Lord 15
Second World War 103
separation women 48
Sheehy Skeffington, Francis 47–8, 110